William T. O'Keefe

LOVE AND NEGOTIATE

Other books by John Scanzoni

Opportunity and the Family

The Black Family in Modern Society

Sexual Bargaining: Power Politics in Marriage

Sex Roles, Life Styles, and Childbearing

Sex Roles, Women's Work, and Marital Conflict

Men, Women, and Change: A Sociology of Marriage and Family (with Letha Scanzoni)

LOVE AND NEGOTIATE

CREATIVE CONFLICT IN MARRIAGE

JOHN SCANZONI

WORD BOOKS
PUBLISHER
WACO, TEXAS

ISBN 0–8499–0100–6
Library of Congress catalog card number: 78–65816
Printed in the United States of America

For Letha—
>
> as we struggle together to keep on
> learning and doing mutual submission
>
> and

For Steve and Dave—

> who wish I'd learned and done a lot
> more of it a lot sooner

CONTENTS

PREFACE

SEVERAL YEARS AGO, it was my privilege to participate in a national conference devoted to discovering "priorities in the family." My particular assignment was to "critique the kind of hierarchical approach to family relationships that is being suggested" by a variety of persons. I was asked to "offer a sound biblically-based alternative." During the months preceding and following that conference, I have been pondering the alternative. This book is the result.

My concern is to help wives and husbands, children and parents learn how to arrive at marriage and family decisions *together*. While the book is mostly about marital conflict, it deals with parent-child conflict as well. In many circles today, a simple formula is touted as *the* biblical basis for conflict-resolution: acknowledge the headship and submit to the leadership of the husband-father. An alternative to that one-way submission is what the Bible calls *mutual* submission, and that's what this book is all about. The question I try to answer is this: How can wives and husbands struggle together to figure out what to do, whether they face routine, in-between, or critical decisions? What is the practical, every-day, "nitty-gritty" meaning of husbands submitting to wives, and wives to husbands?

No one book can do it all. Books such as *All We're Meant to Be; Women, Men and the Bible,*[1] and others help to lay the biblical and theological foundations for equity between the sexes, and thus conflict-resolution based on mutual submission. Since those and similar books are readily available there is no reason for me to repeat what they say. Other titles that deal specifically with conflict-resolution and marital communication and intimacy include *The Intimate Enemy, Alive and Aware,* and *Pairing.*[2] A visit to your local bookseller will reveal many more. What is lacking, however, is a book about marital conflicts that attempts to tie together a Christian alternative to hierarchy with insights from the behavioral and social sciences.

In trying to fill that void, chapters 1 and 2 take a fresh look at biblical perspectives on conflict in general and on marital negotiation in particular. The term *negotiation* is used repeatedly throughout the book. Although at first it may seem a rather cold and forbidding term, we shall see that in reality it is nothing more than the "nuts and bolts" of mutual submission. Chapters 3 through 7 deal with the specifics of marital conflict-resolution and its opposite—deadlocks.

Chapter 8 questions the hierarchical approach to dealing with children, and suggests that mutual submission has application to parent-child as well as husband-wife relations. Chapter 9 also focuses on the premarital period and offers guidelines on how single men and women can negotiate with each other. The idea is to learn how to break the "dating habit" and switch instead to "friending."

Why write a book like this? I believe that any sort of hierarchical approach to marriage in which the man is "head," "leader," or "initiator," and the woman is something else, is going to rob couples of the riches they could otherwise have. The later chapters explain in detail what I mean by that statement. Here let me say that I am convinced marital hierarchy undermines not only the development of deep, intimate friendship, but also the capacity to cope with conflict in the most creative ways possible. Why write this book? So that women and men can have richer marriages.

Kahlil Gibran says it all:

Among intelligent People
The surest basis for marriage
is Friendship,
The Sharing of real interests,
the ability to fight out
ideas together
and understand each other's
thoughts
and dreams.*

* From *Beloved Prophet: The Love Letters of Kahlil Gibran and Mary Haskell, and Her Private Journal,* by Kahlil Gibran and Mary Haskell, ed. Virginia Hilu, p. 408, © 1972 by Alfred A. Knopf, Inc. Used by permission.

1.

FEMALE, MALE, AND CONFLICT

"O.K., WE'VE HEARD about equal-partner marriage, and we're for it. But how does it work? How do we do it? What are *practical* principles for making it work? What about the leadership problem? How do we deal with conflict?" Books like *All We're Meant To Be* and some others spelled out the challenge. Men and women could be equal partners both in marriage and out of it—the Bible makes that clear. But in the years since that book first appeared, people around the country have been asking over and over again: "Can it really be done? In the everyday nitty-gritty of things, can marriages survive without some sort of final (male) head?"

People who raise those questions realize that traditional marriages have no corner on the satisfaction market. Since most marriages remain traditional, it is *traditional* marriages—including all too many Christian marriages—that account for the great majority of divorces. Further, among many Christian marriages that remain stable, it is becoming painfully obvious that all too soon the initial zest and delight in each other is replaced by determination to endure each other and stick it out.

PROPOSED SOLUTIONS

Some Christians are keenly aware of these problems, and a number have attempted to provide answers. According to one solution, Christian wives are advised to take the initiative and jazz up their sex life. They are told that any Christian woman worth her black stockings and see-through negligee should be able to stimulate her husband into coveting her body and thus their marriage. Other Christians have trouble with that approach and cast about for something less sensational. They try to convince us to "go back to the good old days."[1] And what were they like?

As late as the eighteenth century, husbands ruled their households just as kings ruled their countries. Their word was law, and the law was their word. That is, the law gave them almost total power over their wives. The only thing they could *not* do was murder them. Otherwise wives could demand no rights or privileges from their husbands.

The law permitted husbands to beat their wives with impugnity and men were not loath to take advantage of their "rights." For women, the right to divorce was extremely limited, and recent evidence shows that many wives simply deserted their husbands rather than suffer.

Fortunately, in the past 200 years women have gradually been gaining more legal and social rights. The total, unquestioned, uncontested power of husbands is gone forever. Just as 1776 saw the beginning of the end of kings and their inherent royal supremacy, so that same period witnessed the birth pangs of feminism and the beginnings of the end of inherent male supremacy.

Historically, the word *negotiate* was not part of a king's vocabulary. He had only to pontificate and people did his bidding.

It may be quaint to say, "That right went the way of the horse and buggy," but it is interesting to note that both royalty and horse-drawn carriages went their ways about the time of World War I. Even in modern totalitarian states such as the People's Republic of China or the U.S.S.R., leaders must be careful lest they catch a cold, miss a meeting, and find that their peers have voted them into retirement (or worse). In 1974 a president of the United States was forced to resign, essentially because he forgot that modern leaders can no longer pontificate.

By the same token, husbands once had the privilege to pontificate, and to negotiate was something quite foreign. It still is foreign to a lot of men and women, and some Christians want to keep it that way. Since the "sex as ploy" solution doesn't fit their style, they want to maintain the idea that the husband has final and unquestioned authority over his wife and children. Some of them argue that there is a divinely established chain of command much like that in the Army through which the general instructs the colonel who instructs the lieutenant who instructs "the troops." In the family, it is God over the husband over the wife over the children.

Other voices for this view add variations here and there to make it seem less onerous. But all of them are consistent in arguing that the divinely ordained way to have healthy families and strong churches is to "put the man back in his rightful place as the head of the family." To be sure, the modern husband should not be the stern, unapproachable despot of yesteryear, although many Christians once believed that that sort of male demeanor pleased God and was a sign of deep spirituality. The husband may "discuss" things with his wife and children, but if they can't agree on what to do, then he has the God-given "responsibility" (read "right") to exercise his leadership in a "loving" manner. And the wife and children? They have the equally God-given responsibility (read "duty") to obey.

MALE AUTHORITY AND CREATIVE CONFLICT

That theology has been evaluated elsewhere[2] and in later chapters we will look at it more closely. I do not believe that is the only biblical position. Just as there are equally devout saints who have different views on baptism, the Lord's Supper, church government, and so forth, in the same way there are equally devout Christians who differ over the roles of women and men in marriage, church, and society. The point I want to introduce now is one I shall emphasize repeatedly in later chapters: *Persons who accept a hierarchical view of marriage will never be able to negotiate effectively or engage in creative conflict with their spouses.*

In fact, that principle holds for any relationship. When kings were in vogue, their subjects did not know how to talk to them creatively, that is, in a way that would turn out best for everyone. The development of the English Parliament (the forerunner of the U.S. Congress) represented a struggle that took place over hundreds of years to learn how to resolve differences between king and people. The kings took Romans 13: 1–4 very seriously: God appointed them to rule over the people; therefore the people had to obey. As long as kings felt that way, they had little inclination to negotiate. And as long as the people knew that kings felt that way, where was the incentive to try?

Similarly, if husbands feel that they have some kind of God-given prerogative to be the "head," then they are not likely to undertake the painful and difficult process of learning how to negotiate in genuine fashion with their wives. As one preacher put it, "A good woman is like an echo—she speaks only when spoken to; but not like an echo in that she never has the last word." The fact that in the back of their minds husbands know that they have the "last word" is going to undermine any efforts to bargain in earnest. And on the other side, Christian married women soon recognize that it really doesn't do much good to learn to negotiate if their husbands feel that way about headship. Negotiation is hard work and, like the tango, it takes two. There simply is no incentive to try to do that hard work if at bottom it is merely a game. It's like the days in which, if the king didn't like what the Parliament was doing, he'd simply dissolve it and send the members home. Knowing that her husband can dissolve their negotiations by virtue of his headship discourages many Christian women from taking serious part in them and working through creative conflict.

Women Who Fail to Resist

This kind of discouragement can work two ways. The first and most obvious way is that it keeps women from resisting their husbands when they feel they're wrong. Recall that Jesus rebuked his disciples for seeking power (Matt. 20: 25–28). He told them that nonbelievers seek to control others for their own benefit. That kind of power, implied Jesus, corrupts both the user and the used. Instead, said Jesus, the true servant of God seeks to be the servant of others. But throughout the Bible God's servants can be found resisting unchecked power that had become corrupt: Moses versus Pharaoh; David versus Saul; the prophets versus the kings of Judah and Israel; Jesus himself versus the Pharisees. The early Christian martyrs resisted (often in blood) Roman efforts to suppress their worship. Later, dissenting Christians had to resist the unfair powers of the church (first Catholic, then Protestant) to suppress their convictions about how God wanted them to speak and live in the world. Certainly a central theme of Scripture and one that pervades all of church history is that Christians are to resist wrong as they understand it.

As far as wives are concerned, this means that when they believe their husbands are wrong, or in need of constructive suggestions or some sort of consultation, they have the *responsibility* to talk to them about it. (Later chapters will show that there are no matters in which wives should hesitate to speak up. There are no non-negotiable issues, whether they involve money, or sex, or children, or the woman's own interests, or a move, or in-laws, or church involvement, or any other.) Because men have had unchecked power for so many thousands of years, they have a tendency at the very least to use it to excess, and at the worst to have been corrupted by it and through it to hurt other family members.[3]

Disraeli's observation that "power corrupts and absolute power corrupts absolutely" has its definite application in marriage. Because husbands are not accustomed to correction, they too easily become selfish at the expense of wife and children. And if their wives do not "exhort and rebuke" them, who will? But wives who know that their husbands are going to have the final word are less likely to resist their husbands. Past frustrations will lead them to feel that resistance is next to useless, that very often their husbands don't take them seriously. Even if a wife protests and asserts, "I believe this is God's will in this matter," the husband can always respond with a counterassertion: "I see God's will differently, and since someone has to resolve the problem, it has to be me."

But what if he's wrong?—wrong in his perception of God's will, wrong in what he's doing? Many Christians have admitted to being wrong about discerning God's will in matters outside the family. But rare is the husband who admits that about family decisions. Why? How serious is it that husbands are sometimes wrong?

There's a framed sign behind the manager's desk of the New York Yankees. It reads: "Company Rules. Rule No. 1: The Boss is always right. Rule No. 2: If the Boss is wrong, see

Rule 1." [4] As anyone who follows organized sports knows, how lightheartedly or grimly to take that motto depends on one thing—winning. If the coach or manager is winning games, everyone has a good laugh over it. If he's losing, it's no joke, because he'll soon be out of a job. After all, owners are the boss's boss, and they consider losing a very serious matter. But if wives are merely "players," they're caught in a *Catch 22* by the rules: "The boss is right; if he's wrong, he's right anyway." How should wives react to that situation, especially if it happens that he's wrong too often? I'll come back to that question in later chapters. Right now the point is that male headship keeps women from their God-given responsibility to check men when they use power to do things women feel are not right, or are not pleasing to God.

Women Who Fail to Initiate

A second way that male headship discourages women from creative conflict is more subtle, yet perhaps more serious than the first—certainly more tragic. We've all heard husbands (or wives) say, "We never have conflicts where I'm forced to make the final decision"; or, "Things just never get that serious in our marriage"; or, "We always manage to work things out." Others, speaking of their own or often of their parents' marriages, will assert, "We (they) never had a fight in our (their) lives." The assumption underlying these statements and many others like them is that *the absence of conflict is healthy* or *the sure sign of a strong, healthy marriage.* Later on, we'll pursue in greater detail just whether or not conflict is healthy, but right now let's make it clear that its absence can mean many things besides health. Not having pain in no way guarantees that a body is physically sound! Not having any or much marital negotiation and/or conflict can mean that either partner has become bland, reticent, passive, and lethargic in suggesting changes in ways to improve marriage, to make it healthier and better.

A few pages ago we saw that male headship keeps the woman from being a negative force, resisting where it is necessary. She can also be kept from being a positive force—contributing ideas for change and participating fully in carrying them out. For example, all of us can think back to the time when we were in school and recall single women who were vigorous, keen, insightful persons—full of ideas and energy. They participated in the same projects and activities as men students, often as editors, leaders, chairpersons, etc. They asserted themselves; they were taken seriously. They contributed ideas and plans that were weighed on their own merits, not on the sex of the originator. Suggestions flowed freely; there were discussions and disagreements; and what emerged were plans that almost everybody in the group could live with.

Over the years, some of these women have remained single and we meet them at alumni gatherings, or elsewhere. Most of them are still as vigorous as before. They have had to spend their lives in businesses, mission fields, offices, churches, factories, schools as contributing persons. They have had to keep on learning about how to hammer out differences of opinion—how to negotiate and compromise. Their ideas, while in general perhaps not taken as seriously as those of male coworkers, are nonetheless listened to with some attention, depending on their position. They have had continuing experience since school of influencing the ways things turn out, and they show it with an air of confidence and self-assurance that is often lacking in many married women, especially Christians.

Regardless of how self-assured and autonomous women were prior to marriage, once they are under the umbrella of male headship those characteristics gradually diminish in significance. Women can now *depend* on their husbands, not only for material provision, but for family leadership. Consequently, since it is no longer appreciated and/or needed, the reservoir of creative and innovative ideas that came tumbling out while they were single slowly dries up. It's not that husbands of good-will consciously suppress their wives' creative energies (though some husbands do); it's simply that (1) husbands fail to stir up and mine ideas from their wives on how better to arrange their marriages and families; (2) husbands fail to treat wives' ideas as seriously as their own—to put them into the crucible of negotiation to see how they meld with their own. A vicious cycle results: Over the years, women find their ideas and suggestions are not reinforced by their husbands. Less reinforcement causes them to make fewer creative inputs. Fewer inputs means fewer opportunities for their husbands to reinforce them. And so the cycle continues.

The long-range consequence is that, if couples stick it out, by the time they are in their thirties the once-dynamic woman has unobtrusively faded away—not into the woodwork—but into her husband. She has ceased to be her own person and is now merely his extension, his "missus," his wife, his shadow. Is she then going to negotiate aggressively with her husband? Is she going to press for them to find new ways to relate to each other? to their children? to friends? to church? to God? Not likely, and not because he necessarily actively suppresses her, but simply because the whole style of their lives has led them to that convenient and somnolent arrangement. She no longer contributes actively to marital decision-making simply because she has never been rewarded for trying it. Indeed, years earlier, when she was still trying to be that kind of whole person, she may have been punished for it in the sense that her ideas were ignored, minimized, or perhaps even ridiculed. Or they may have been subject to the greatest putdown of all: "Dear, though you may see it differently, I believe this is what God wants us to do."

Hierarchy—The Wave of Yesterday

Recall that we got into this discussion of how hierarchical views of male headship impede negotiation and creative conflict by stating that some Christians want to go back to hierarchy. Those who want to go back fail to realize how stifling it is to the creative energies of both partners—creative energies that could go into making *healthier* marriages. But besides failing to see that, advocates of hierarchy also fail to realize that they are riding a wave of the past.

In chapter 2 we will examine the biblical basis for negotiation based on *equality* of the sexes. In other words, it is possible to interpret the Bible to support a hierarchical view, but it is also possible to interpret it to support an egalitarian view. Which view you become persuaded of depends on a variety of factors, just as you are persuaded that baptism by immersion is more or less preferable to sprinkling, or that being a charismatic Christian is more or less pleasing to God than not being one.

Many Amish people believe that God wants Christians to dress in seventeenth-century clothes, but the number who agree with that doctrine is probably declining every year. There are some Christians who believe the Bible compels footwashing, but most do not concur. Up until just a few decades ago Protestant Christians believed that birth control as well as abortion was prohibited by the Bible. But today few Protestants (and not all lay Catholics) believe that birth control is sinful. What happened? Did the Bible change? Of course not. What happened was that that interpretation of birth control simply became untenable in the light of changing social conditions, especially the great shifts from farm to city. That is, Protestant and Catholic theologians had uniformly agreed that the Bible prohibits birth control. But the laity (and clergy) began to use birth control anyhow, because of economic and social pressures. In response to what the people were doing, theologians at first began to say less and less about it. Later on, they reversed themselves completely and told us birth control is a *good* thing—that God wants us to be responsible parents and not have more children than we can afford.

The fact is that that very same kind of process is already underway—and has been so for some years—in Christian families with regard to hierarchy. The kinds of social conditions under which we live inevitably undermine hierarchical views of marriage. Civil rights laws, for instance, guarantee equal educational and occupational opportunities to women. Women's sports gain ever more money and attention in high schools, colleges, and at the professional ranks. Women become prominent at all levels of government—in England a woman stands ready to become prime minister. Increasing numbers of women are being ordained as clergy. And not only is hierarchy crumbling outside the family, it is gradually collapsing within it as well.

Two separate essays by Fritz Ridenour provide a vivid illustration of the gradual evolution that is steadily occurring in many Christian families. In January 1975, he wrote an essay called, "Let's not be glib about Lib." [5] He says, "The Bible . . . is 'pro-men's leadership.' . . . Women don't need liberating; they need leading and loving. . . ." Ridenour presented in this essay an "enlightened" evangelical position on women's and men's roles, but it remained a variation on the theme of hierarchy, and thus has the same negative effects just discussed. Throughout the essay Ridenour came across as quite sure of his views and somewhat condescending toward women: "Men are still tops in twisting caps off bottles, changing tires in the rain, and keeping the bed warm on cold nights." He was certain male leadership would promote healthy marriages.

Let's flash ahead to February 1978. Things have changed in the Ridenour household—his wife, Jackie, has taken a full-time job outside the home. [6] Nowhere in this second essay do we unearth pious soundings about male leadership. Instead, what we discover is what we'll be talking about in chapter 3—plenty of forthright bargaining between husband and wife. Moreover, it is the wife, Jackie, who is taking the initiative and suggesting ways Fritz should change by participating more fully in household chores. In these negotiations, she is doing the leading, he is doing the following. And as he conforms to Jackie's wishes about these chores, he says, "The hardest part, perhaps, is to redefine the old husband/wife roles that we have both played for years."

Instead of proclaiming "leadership," meaning differences in rights, rewards, and responsibilities, he now talks about *teamwork,* which implies equality of rights, rewards, and responsibilities. "She works at the office, I work at the office; she works at home, I work at home. To put it another way, if she is expected to put in forty hours a week on the job, we'd be a better team in *all* respects, housework included. And like any other good team we need to back each other up, help each other, encourage each other."

Fritz no longer implies that he has the final answer about male/female roles and marital decision-making. He's now struggling along with the rest of us. He seems to have come a long way from the views of the advocates of male headship and female submission. I have a strong suspicion that in hundreds of other Christian homes many subtle, low-key, unannounced, unheralded changes are also taking place. Those husbands and wives don't bother to shout pro or con about women's lib or even ERA. They simply realize that as women begin to serve God fully and freely with all their talents, men are beginning to cooperate with them in this new and exciting wave of tomorrow. Like Fritz, more and more Christian men are coming to realize that while the changes are by no means easy to carry out, they are better than hierarchy, both in the short run and in the long run. The changes are better for women, for men, for children and families, and for church and society.

Underlying these profound changes in marriage/family is the position of women in society. Increasing educational and job opportunities, political visibility, athletic accomplishments—the whole tenor of modern societies is moving inexorably toward equal footing among all human beings—women and men, blacks and whites, rich and poor. It will be many decades before anything fully approaching those goals is realized, but the trend is there and it is irreversible. It has been spilling over into the family for years, especially as more and more women enter vocations. Some Christian women have already been asserting themselves, in the attempt to have creative negotiation and conflict with their husbands. *Their numbers are going to increase in the future, as are the numbers of Christian men who are willing to give up ancient male prerogatives.*

Some Christians might respond by saying that this is just another instance of following the world, or the society around us. "There ought to be some Christian distinctives somewhere," they say, "and we ought to draw the line on the matter of male leadership. Just because they're doing it doesn't mean we have to!" This is not a book on the history of changes in Christian ethics, so I am not responding to that problem in depth. Briefly, what Christians have to be able to do is to identify God's working in society and respond to it. For example, few Christians today would doubt that birth control is a gift of God that brings about healthier families. Yet not too many years ago most Christians said, "That's following the world." They failed to see that God was working to provide humankind with that gift. Now most of us see the gift and appreciate it.

I believe the same reasoning applies to changes in the roles of women and men, that God is working to provide a new gift—egalitarian relationships between the sexes. One of the ways we can and must respond is to explore the practical implications on how to make marital decisions. Decision-making was comparatively easy when the male did all the deciding.

It's a lot harder now, but it's also a lot more rewarding, enriching, and *fair*.

This book is not talking about something that might be or could be or should be—the reality is with us right now. Increasing numbers of women and men (especially younger persons) want an egalitarian marriage relationship because they know the old hierarchy simply won't work any more—at least for them (though it may have worked very well for their parents). At the chapter's outset, the question was posed: how do you do it? How do you tell the "boss" he's wrong? If the old answers are untenable and indefensible, how do you deal with marital problems—conflicts, disagreements?

That's what the remaining chapters are all about.

2.

A BIBLICAL BASIS FOR
NEGOTIATION AND CONFLICT

In CHAPTER 1, I used terms such as *negotiation* or *creative conflict* without explicitly describing or defining them. The chapter's main thrust was to make us aware of the distinction between hierarchy or "male leadership," and *something else*. Introducing that something else is the topic of this chapter. The chapter covers three main questions: (1) What do we mean when we talk about negotiation, conflict, bargaining, and related ideas? (2) Why is it that we hesitate to negotiate (or else to have conflict), quite apart from the hierarchical issue considered in chapter 1? (3) What is the biblical basis for negotiation and conflict?

Now, it would be quite tidy if we could keep these three questions separate by dividing the chapter into three parts, like a sermon. But the fact is that the questions are interwoven like the threads of a fine carpet. It is very difficult to treat one without touching on another. Therefore, we have to gaze at the whole carpet to pick out one thread knowing that at the same time we dangle other threads as well.

For example, negotiation can be defined very simply as "a process of give and take between two (or more) parties, aimed at arriving at a solution or compromise in which each gets something, but not all, that each originally wanted." To many of us, that may sound so crass (especially the "taking") that at first reading we are turned off by the idea, and we may hesitate to negotiate, no matter what our views of hierarchy.

Biblical Examples

Yet the Bible is replete with examples of just that very thing. One of the most famous and important biblical patriarchs, Abraham, ("he was called the 'Friend of God'" [James 2: 23]) was a bargainer of the first order. In Genesis 18, for instance, the Lord told Abraham he would destroy Sodom and Gomorrah. Abraham responded, "Surely you would not destroy the cities if as few as fifty 'righteous' people could be found there." The Lord agreed, but then Abraham kept right on bargaining with God by asking him to lower the number of righteous people necessary to avert disaster—forty-five, forty, thirty, twenty, even ten. And the Lord agreed with Abraham's final offer— he would show mercy if ten righteous people could be found.

Abraham's bargaining skills, however, were not always put to the best of uses. In Genesis 12, we are told that while they were living in Egypt he was somehow able to persuade his wife Sarah to pose as his sister. He felt that if it were known she was actually his wife, the king would kill him to get her into his harem. But when Abraham and Sarah lied, the king negotiated with Abraham for Sarah. We are not told what kinds of give-and-take went on between Abraham and Sarah, but we can be pretty sure that Sarah felt she was giving a whole lot more than she was getting. In the end, Abraham probably exerted the kind of male dominance I talked about in chapter 1. Someone had to make a final decision, he thought, so he was willing to sacrifice his wife to save his own neck. And, being a woman, she was the *property* of her husband—not unlike his other possessions —so what could she do?

Moreover, Abraham was getting a great deal from the king in exchange for Sarah—oxen, sheep, donkeys, camels, butlers, and maids (v. 16). Fortunately for Sarah, God intervened and "caused" the king to give her back to Abraham. The king was not terribly happy with Abraham's deceit, however, so he ejected him and all his family from Egypt.

This story marks all the things bargaining should *not* be, and it also underscores why people are often put off by the very term. Abraham was selfish, greedy, underhanded, deceitful, and insensitive. He thought only of himself, not of Sarah or of the king. He thought how splendid it would be to have those animals and servants. He didn't mind lying and cheating to get them. He didn't consider seriously the enormity of the indignities he was perpetrating on Sarah.

We can use Abraham's behavior as the prime example—the polar extreme—of what no one of good will wants in marriage. Unfortunately, men, because of their greater rights and privileges, have, down through the centuries, often treated women in just that same cavalier fashion (though, one hopes, not often to that extreme). A few women, in those rare instances in which they have gotten social advantages, have sometimes dealt with men in precisely this same way. The 16th century English queen known as "Bloody Mary" condemned hundreds of Protestants to death. That sort of cruelty and revenge is totally opposite to what I have in mind. Such behavior starts wars, breaks up trading and business partnerships, and destroys friendships and marriages.

But Abraham must have pondered long and well the lessons and guilt of his dishonest bargaining, because in the very next chapter (Gen. 13) we find him negotiating in a very generous fashion. He and his nephew Lot were nomadic sheiks in Canaan. When their respective herdsmen began fighting over scarce resources of land and water for their animals, Abraham proposed a compromise of the most magnanimous sort. He suggested to Lot that they divide up their clans and their territory. Lot could choose any land area he wanted and take his part of the clan there. Abraham would go in the opposite direction with his clan. That was indeed a most generous offer, and Lot took it. He picked good grazing land with plenty of water and moved there.

In this story Abraham exemplifies a great deal of what negotiation should be. He was honest, forthright, and totally unselfish. Most of all, he deferred to Lot's wishes. He simply said, "Lot, you do what looks best to you, and I'll abide by it."

Furthermore, Abraham, as the oldest male among their clans, could have exercised his ultimate male authority and told Lot, "Someone has to exercise leadership here, and it has to be me." Instead he set aside his prerogatives for Lot's sake. That, incidentally, says a great deal to husbands who feel that family leadership demands that they somehow be ultimately responsible for final decisions. Compromising sometimes means letting the other person decide, even at personal sacrifice or cost.

Today, as in Abraham's day, compromise makes the world go 'round. Government officials compromise; so do business people, and so do church workers and officers. In our everyday lives at work, with our friends, *and at home,* we all have to learn the difficult lesson of "giving in"—of mutual submission. Some Christians think compromise is a "dirty word." They associate compromise with bending to evil or error. And, of course, should someone ask us to compromise one of the Ten Commandments, we would have to resist. But on most other things in life compromise is essential for smooth-running relationships. Let us say, for instance, that a certain mission board has a policy that missionaries should not marry until one year after engagement. Some officials think they should keep the rule as is; others want to abolish it entirely. Finally, someone suggests they change it to a six-month waiting period. Both sides give up their original ideas, agree to this change, and so the important work of the mission can go on.

The Matter of Justice

Talking about cost or giving in raises an important question. How much did Abraham actually sacrifice in deferring to Lot's judgment? The text (v. 2) tells us he was very rich both in animals and servants. He had so much more than Lot he felt he could afford to be as generous as he was. I do not mean to be cynical or snide about Abraham when I point this out. Indeed, many other men in his position have been greedy to get even more possessions. They have squashed their relatives and taken over their lands, livestock, and possessions. It was good that Abraham was as magnanimous as he was; it would have been terribly unjust had he done otherwise. Jesus said, "To whom much is given, of him much is required" (Luke 12: 48). In part, it was because he had so much that he was able to deal with Lot as he did.

Recall Jesus' parable of the man who was forgiven by another man of the sizable debt that he owed him (Matt. 18: 23–35). But then that first man turned around and threw a third man into debtor's prison because he could not pay a small debt. When the one who had forgiven him his huge debt heard it, he was infuriated, because of the gross injustice. He then had the unjust man punished.

Or remember the story the prophet Nathan told King David: A poor man had only one tame sheep, but one day his rich neighbor who had great flocks of sheep stole the poor man's one sheep (2 Sam. 12). David became exceedingly angry, and ordered fourfold restitution of the slain sheep. David, of course, was the man. Even though King David had several wives and concubines he nonetheless had a hankering for the wife of one of his army officers. He then had an affair with her, got her pregnant, and made sure her husband was killed so that he could add her to his collection. But in spite of anything else that could be said about David, he could get angry at injustice once he saw it, including his own. Unfortunately in this instance there was little he could do to rectify his gross injustices.

Jesus became equally angry at injustice. In addition to the many parables in which he often condemned injustice or unfairness are his own words to the religious leaders in Matthew 23. The whole tenor of that passage is set in verse 4: the leaders lay heavy burdens on others, but they themselves will do nothing to help carry them. "How unfair that is," Jesus is saying. Throughout the chapter, Jesus' anger with their many injustices is obvious, exploding when he pronounces "woes" on them, calls them "hypocrites," whitewashed tombs, snakes, and so on. While excoriating their injustices, he reminds them of their ancestors' injustices in killing the prophets. And why did they kill the prophets? Because, among other things, the prophets had pointed out the injustices that were being perpetrated by the rich against the poor, the kings and nobles against the common folk (see 1 Kings 21).

From Genesis to Revelation, the Scriptures place a great deal of emphasis upon *justice*. We have just looked at some examples of treating others fairly in our day-to-day relationships. The Old Testament prophets, David, and Jesus were very concerned that the rich were *taking* a great deal from the poor and giving them very little in return. We are outraged today by unscrupulous salesmen who prey upon unsuspecting elderly citizens. The salesman comes to the door, promises them a new roof, takes their money and then, if he returns at all, he provides inferior materials and shoddy workmanship.

During Old Testament times the privileged people were more

direct than most contemporary salesmen. They harmed the poor by taking their lands, putting them in jail, and even murdering them. Micah cries out to the rich, "What does God require of you, O man, but to do *justice!*" (6: 8). In this sense justice means giving what you should to others, and not taking what you shouldn't. To be just is to be fair, to be *equitable.*

Micah adds further that the ancient Jews were also to *love kindness.* (The RSV margin suggests: "love steadfast love.") In a very real sense, kindness and love go an important step beyond justice or fairness. Love implies giving more than you should, or are obligated to do. That's an important issue, and we'll return to it later.

A second way justice is used in Scripture is the common theology of many Christians. The idea is that a holy God had to be just in punishing the sins of humankind, but out of love, he sent Jesus Christ to bear that punishment. Thus God exhibits his love and justice, both at the same time. There is therefore an intimate theological connection between justice and love, just as there is a close experiential connection between the two in the Micah passage.

Third, justice is also at the core of a grand biblical theme that has its culmination in the Book of Revelation. We all know only too well that the world contains innumerable injustices and unfairnesses—the wicked prosper, the good suffer; evil triumphs, generosity is overcome by greed; innocent children and adults suffer from disease, famine, war, genocide, unemployment, death, and the plain heartaches of daily living. Yet Christians believe that the promise of the Christ in Isaiah 9: 7 means that at his second coming, he will "set things straight." Though we do not know *how* he will do it, we believe that all injustices will finally be ended, and persons will ultimately receive their just deserts.

These three scriptural uses of justice (treating others *fairly* in the here and now, Christ's redemptive work, and Christ's ultimate triumph over evil) demonstrate clearly what an important quality it is for the Christian to understand and to pursue.

The most immediate application of justice to our lives is, of course, the first of the three. Used in that sense, a more precise term is *equity,* meaning simply that we should be fair with others and they should be fair with us.

What Is Fair?

But what is "fair?" Jesus answered that question in the verse known as The Golden Rule: "Do for others just what you want them to do for you" (Luke 6: 31, TEV). If the roof salesman had taken that injunction seriously, he would not have treated the senior citizens the way he did.

Trying to decide what is fair, and what is not fair is not always a simple matter. To take a very common example, many organized sports almost yearly make some changes in their rules about what is or is not fair. And the players have to change their habits so as to "play fair."

Not only in sports but indeed in all phases of life a great deal of what is fair or unfair cannot be written in a rule book or into a code of law. Most of life is guided by unwritten agreements between people as to how to treat each other fairly. Many of these unwritten agreements are often arrived at by tacit or implicit negotiation. Some things are simply "understood." Many other agreements may even have existed long before the persons involved ever met each other. But they have learned that certain behaviors have been accepted for some time as fair, and so they do them. Take, for example, traditional dating patterns. A boy is supposed to ask the girl, provide the car and bear its expenses, and also pay for the costs of, say, a movie and snack. Is it fair for him to have to come up with all that money? Until recently, no one ever gave such a question much thought; and if they did, they certainly would not characterize that long-standing custom as unfair. Dating customs were something that most people simply understood as being fair and therefore right, "the thing to do." Few people would have thought it was right or fair for a girl to have to do those things for a boy. (See chapter 8 in which we question those customs.)

But whether there are "understood" agreements or whether we have to reach an *understanding* with people (for example, who among several persons arriving at the same instant go first into a revolving door; or which of four cars arriving simultaneously at a four-way stop sign should first pass through the intersection), the Golden Rule should be our standard of fairness: "I want to treat others in just exactly the same way I want them to treat me."

Fairness through Negotiation

Now, if we think of *negotiation* as the way to arrive at these understandings or agreements based on the Golden Rule's standard of fairness, then it is no longer a nasty word. It is not something we shun or shy away from, but instead, something we want to learn to do, and do better all the time. Seen in that light, negotiation is not crass or reprehensible. It is not a means for greedy grasping or self-agrandizement, but an important means to help make human relations fair and just and equitable. And when human relations are fair, they are clearly pleasing to God, since justice pleases him; it is part of his nature and his own sovereign working in the world.

Mutual Submission as Negotiation

In Christian terms, negotiation is the practical outworking in marriage, and outside it also, of what has recently become a very widely discussed idea—the practice of "mutual submission." In Ephesians 5: 21, Paul tells all Christians to "be subject to one another." But how can that be done? In the story above, should Lot have been subject to Abraham, or he to Lot? How does a husband know when to be subject to his wife, or the wife to the husband?

The answers to these questions are easy to say but very difficult to do—mutual submission has to be negotiated. Sometimes one party has to make most of the concessions, sometimes the other party has to do so. Most often, if mutual submission is to become a reality, each party has to make some concessions. (Remember our story of the missionary society and their disagreement over how long engagements should last: each side had to "give in" or concede a little to the other; each side had to submit to the other.) This book is actually a primer on the art of mutual submission—practical suggestions on how family members can go on "giving in" to each other. In marriage, it is the day-to-day practice of mutual submission that demonstrates the love spouses say they have for each other. It is those kinds of practical compromises that result in fairness and justice.

Love and Justice

I was once speaking about the import of justice in connection with changes in husband-wife relations when a man in the congregation promptly shot up and said he *loved* his wife, and that love was a far greater thing than justice or being fair with her. Taken at face value no one could disagree with that statement. Love is going the second mile, beyond the first mile, which is *justice*. But as I answered the gentleman, most husbands haven't actually yet gone the first mile, to say nothing of the second. Recall that Paul said, "The greatest . . . is love" (1 Cor. 13). In that chapter, and throughout the Scriptures, love is defined in terms of giving, doing, serving: God loved, he gave; if we love, we are to serve. For instance, it could be said that

Abraham loved Lot so much that he gave up his own rights, and indeed I'm sure that's true. Love and justice are inseparable—they are two sides of the same coin.

But then someone asks, if love is giving, how can it have anything to do with negotiation, which I defined as giving *and taking*? Doesn't the the spiritual Christian say, "I love, I do not take. I do not want or expect anything in return. I simply give and keep on giving. I do not expect submission from my partner." In the words of the hymn, I believe we should "spend and be spent."[1] For instance, in the same passage as The Golden Rule, Jesus tells us to "love our enemies" and to "lend and expect nothing back" (Luke 6: 35).

Women and Justice

This perspective on love has certainly characterized Christian wives down through the centuries. They have loved, and sacrificed, and spent, and given their all to their husbands and to their children. With very little murmur or complaint they have borne endless numbers of children (and many died doing so). They have nurtured those children and supported their husbands with comfort and encouragement. They have expected nothing in return. To be sure, they kept going because of the intrinsic satisfactions coming from the conviction that they were doing God's will. And I believe that God was very cognizant of their efforts and rewarded them both on earth and finally in heaven for their faithful labors.

But in what concrete ways did (do) husbands love their wives (and children, their mothers)? They may have had great *feelings* of warmth toward them, but I am reminded of James 2 where Christians are condemned for merely having feelings of warmth toward others but not *doing* anything about it. Feelings by themselves are an inadequate indicator of love—*actions* prove that love. As our then ten-year-old son once said in family devotions, "Love is a feel-act." Love involves both feelings and actions. (See p. 47 for a "family decision" that asks where and how love and mutual submission can be expressed by both husband and wife.)

The Obligation to Serve

Throughout his letters, Paul repeatedly urges his readers to love and serve God *because* of all God has done for them (Rom. 12: 1–2). He also tells them they are to love and serve others *for the same reason,* because of God's past goodness to them. In Romans 1: 14 he calls himself a *debtor* to people; he owes it to them to present the Good News. How did Paul get to be their debtor? By being in debt to God—and the only way to discharge the debt was to preach to them.

An illustration of what Paul means here is familiar to all who live in the snow belt. If someone's car is stuck in the snow, total strangers will stop and help push his/her car out of the snow. When I asked a college student why that is so, he said, "When I get stuck someone always stops and helps me. I owe it to people who are stuck to do the same for them, even though I've never seen them before and may never see them again."

After Paul preached to those people, and some of them were converted, he continually impressed them with their obligations to God, to others, to him. Paul expected a great deal from them indeed. While he refused material recompense when he lived in their cities, he let it be known that they had an *obligation* to meet material needs where they exist (see 2 Cor. 8).

Moreover, he was overjoyed when he did receive gifts from them while in prison (Phil. 4: 10). He expected that, in every way, their behavior would please God, and thus be rewarding to him personally. Their behavior would show that he had not "labored in vain," but that there was indeed a harvest for his efforts. Paul would often say, "It's because I love you that I want to see some certain behaviors in you . . . that's why I expect it from you . . . it's for your own good . . . if you do it you'll be rewarded both now and in heaven!"

In brief, there was no separation in Paul's mind between his love for them and what he wanted from them. *He did not "spend and become spent" for nothing.* What he wanted was their spiritual well-being so that they could both serve God and be rewarded for doing it. And he also wanted and expected from God, and from them, the rewards of fruitful service now, and eternal rewards from God in heaven.

Certainly every parent, every teacher, anyone who has ever had to make some investment of time and energy to train someone else knows this feeling. You want to see some results, and there's nothing wrong or spiritually immature about that. To be sure, some missionaries, for instance, never see any results and they have to struggle with that, because they would surely like to!

God's Design for Humanity

Paul lived and taught the way he did because *he believed that was exactly the way God deals with humankind.* Look back at Luke 6: 35. Jesus tells us there to expect nothing from those to whom we give and adds that if we do that, *God will reward us greatly.* In verse 38 he says, "Give to others and God will give to you." In both Jesus and Paul, the strong motivation for us to give unstintingly to others is that, as a result of our giving, God will reward us "beyond measure" (v. 38). The theme of reward also permeates the Old Testament, there involving *material* blessing as well.

Though that material theme is missing from the New Testament, the principle of God's rewarding us for selfless service is bound up in the warp and woof of the Gospels and the Epistles (see 1 Cor. 3: 12–15; 2 Tim. 4: 8). For example, in Luke 14:

28–33, Jesus makes it clear that no one should follow him unless they have calculated both the costs and the rewards that are involved in doing so. He tells us to "give up all we have," but to motivate us to do that he tells us that we shall receive in return ten thousand percent interest on our investment in his mission (Matt. 19: 29). In Matthew 16: 26, Jesus tells us very plainly that we should think about *profit,* and what we have to give in order to gain. It's a poor bargain, he says, to gain the whole world, but give up one's life to get it. The KJV uses the very contemporary term *exchange* to describe what Jesus is saying. What should one *exchange* for her/his life? What negotiations should one carry out when one is dealing with the scope, meaning, and thrust of one's entire life? This is not the place to try to deal with the answers to such weighty questions. The point is that counting rewards and costs—thinking very hard about what one has to give up and about what one will get—seems to be intrinsic to God's relationships with humankind.

Future Rewards

In other words, there are at least two reasons why we serve God. One is Paul's idea of moral obligation: Because God loved us and has already dealt so generously with us, we are in his debt to discharge that obligation with loving service to him and to others. But, besides what he has done for us in the *past,* he gives *present* rewards and promises *future* ones. Thus we are surrounded by rewards on all sides and are forced to echo the Psalmist's cry, "What shall I render to the Lord for all his benefits to me?" (116: 12).

God deals with humankind on the basis of continual giving out of his infinite treasury; there is no limit to what he can and does give. But at the same time, God *fully expects* that we will in return give to him: ourselves—our minds, bodies, talents, energies. He expects *reciprocity,* and in moments of greatest spiritual sensitivity, we gladly render him all the loving obedience of which we are capable. But the sad fact is that all Christians fall far short of that kind of reciprocity. We struggle and falter and fail, and then ask forgiveness, saying with Paul, "This one thing I do—I strive toward the goal for the prize of the high calling of God in Christ Jesus."

The Absence of Mutual Submission

Since it is true that we often fail God so miserably, it is even more true we very often fail one another. We do not love as we should; we become selfish, indifferent, greedy, even exploitative. We saw in chapter 1 that this has been especially true in the ways husbands have treated wives. If all Christians loved one another with the "perfect love" that the Scriptures proclaim, then, as John Wesley said, there would be no sin; there would indeed be perfection. Everyone—spouses, parents, children—would be giving to *each other* in the ways Jesus described in Luke 6. If everyone were *giving* in that fashion, no one would ever have to think about *receiving*. Everyone would have everything they needed in the way of spiritual, mental, emotional, material, and opportunity benefits. And in their giving, everyone would be sensitive enough to others to know when their gifts were no longer needed or wanted, so as not to embarrass the recipient.

Negotiation as Discipline

Unfortunately, that ideal situation has not yet been attained because of human frailty. However, the discipline imposed by negotiation aimed at justice can indeed be a way to teach us more of what that ideal situation could be; negotiation can actually move us closer to it. Far better to recognize the realities of our sinfulness and of our tendency to exploit—to tell it the way it is—and then to face up to it through the nitty-gritty of bargaining, than to pull our pharisaical robes around us and cry out, "I am holier than thou because I eschew negotiation; that is too crass. Instead I love!" In the long run love is more likely to be manifested where persons openly negotiate and work at mutual submission than where they hide their heads in the sands of a self-righteous denial of the need to negotiate. People who do that are likely to be in one of two situations: Either they are controlling a situation and don't want it threatened by the changes that negotiation brings (the husband comfortably ensconced as the head of the household); or else they are *controlled* and fearful of the changes that might come should they assert themselves and press for fairness (the submissive wife comfortably ensconced as her husband's helpmeet).

The Limits of Giving

The same Jesus who told his disciples to "keep on giving" also told them that when persons would not accept their gifts they should stop giving and leave them alone (Matt. 10: 14). They were to "shake the dust off their feet" as a symbol that they had indeed fulfilled their obligation, and now they no longer needed to have anything to do with them; they could go to others who had not yet had a chance to receive the disciples' gifts. This was Jesus' way of instructing them as to how to put into practice his earlier words: "Don't cast your pearls before swine" (Matt. 7: 6). Unlike God, human beings do not have infinite intangible or tangible resources to give. In recent years, for instance, research has made us painfully aware of how many battered wives there actually are in the United States. Some of these wives continue to live with their husbands, even though they and their children are constantly being abused by them, because they feel their husbands *need* them. Perhaps these wives feel they can help their husbands in spite of how their husbands treat them. The question is, how long can these women go on being drained before they have no more to give?

Apparently Jesus himself did not intend his words about giving (expecting nothing except reward from God) to be taken to mean that no limits should *ever* be placed on our giving to other people. In Matthew 23: 37 Jesus himself said to the people of Jerusalem, "I wanted to treat you the way a mother hen treats her chicks, but you wouldn't let me do it." Similarly, numerous times during Paul's missions, when he and his message were not wanted in one city, he didn't keep on giving his gifts. As recorded in Acts, he simply moved on to another place to try to find people who would be receptive, who would *respond* to him and to Christ in the ways he wanted them to.

When people will not receive our inputs, how much sense does it make to keep on making them? Or if the inputs we make are doing others more harm than good, shouldn't we stop making them? All adults know that children cannot and should not be given everything they desire. God does *not* give his people all they pray for, but only what, in his sovereign wisdom, he deems to be best. Furthermore, most Christians have always believed that even God's eternal love has limits, precisely because of the justice dimension we discussed earlier. That is, a person who refuses God's forgiveness throughout his lifetime may not be able to presume on his mercy after death. In classical Christian theology, even God's patience and love, and his willingness to forgive apparently have boundaries.[2]

Quite obviously humans are not omniscient, any more than they have infinite resources. Thus it seems to me that the general principle to be drawn from the foregoing is that Christians must exercise wisdom and discretion in knowing how much to give of themselves, for two basic reasons. One, they may give so much as to have nothing left; they may deplete themselves entirely. Two, their giving may do more harm than good to others.

Up to this time many Christian wives have ignored this principle of discretion (which underlies mutual submission) because they believed it was spiritual and pious to do so. Having given much to their husbands but generally having received little that would affirm their own autonomy and personhood, they became drained as a result. Second, because women gave and expected nothing in return, many men learned to be selfish or at least indifferent in their dealings with women. Women, in other words, really did men no service through their humble subjection.

A Biblical Example of Mutual Submission

The principle of "wisdom and discretion"—of expecting *mutual* giving—is clearly biblical and is vividly illustrated in Acts 6. These earliest Christians—Jews and Hellenists (the latter were Greek-speaking Jews who had formerly lived outside of Palestine)—were now living together in communal fashion (Acts 2: 44–45). They held no private property, but instead contributed to a common pool out of which the needs of all were to be met. Evidently the Jewish Christians must have controlled the outputs of daily food, because in verse 1 we are told that the Hellenists complained against the Jews because the Hellenist widows were not getting enough food. In spite of the fact that they were all Christians, the Jews native to Palestine evidently retained their traditionally negative feelings about Jews who had been living among Gentiles, even though they had now become Christians.

What should the Hellenists do? They could keep quiet about it, and suffer loss of food in silence. (That is exactly what many Christian women have done and do with regard to their husbands. They suffer in silence "and love" in order to keep the peace, and to show "they are in subjection.") But the Hellenists believed it wasn't *fair* for the Jews to get more food than they. After all, they contributed just as much (everything they had) as did the Jews. What was the role of love here? Some would argue that if the Hellenists really loved the Jews, they'd let them have the food—that God would somehow make it up to them either in this life or in the next. On the other hand, an even stronger argument can be made that if the Jews really loved the Hellenists they would never have shortchanged them in the first place. And even more to the point, when it was brought to the Jews' attention that they were actually hurting the Hellenists, love should have dictated that they immediately stop doing so. But they did not stop, and that is why the conflict escalated to such a degree that the twelve Apostles had to deal with it (v. 2). Clearly, the Jews were not being loving. Therefore if the Hellenists had kept quiet they would have allowed the Jews to continue in their unloving—sinful—ways. (And, as painful as it is to say it, when Christian wives "keep quiet" they may very well be allowing their husbands to continue in their unloving—sinful—ways.)

In such a situation, it is best to speak up and point out that the other party is being unfair. *The Hellenists did more spiritual good for the Jews by challenging them than by keeping still.* And evidently the twelve Apostles agreed with the Hellenists— the Jews were indeed being unfair and thus by definition, unloving. By pointing out this injustice the Hellenists were pleasing God and helping the church to be stronger, so to end the conflict the Apostles negotiated a compromise. Apparently the Hellenists wanted the Apostles to distribute the food. The Apostles' response in verse 2 is highly instructive: "It is not *reason* (KJV) that we should leave the word of God and serve tables." Both the RSV and TEV translate it: "It is not *right* . . .". In effect the Apostles said, "It is not reasonable, right, or fair for us to distribute food and cut back our preaching time."

Now one could argue that if the Apostles really loved the Hellenists and the Jews, they would have been glad to give of themselves in this way—by serving. Weren't the Apostles being selfish in refusing? Did they think they were "too good" for such routine work? But their response was that *they had only limited time and energies,* and they believed that God wanted them to devote their gifts and talents to preaching and prayer (v. 4). So instead the Apostles proposed a creative compromise that would get them out of a task they felt was unfair. And it apparently pleased both the Hellenists and the Jews: "Let the church pick out seven capable men to distribute the food." That was done and it turned out that all seven were Hellenists. Presumably they would guarantee that Hellenist people would get their fair share because they themselves were Hellenists; but at the same time they would go to great lengths not to short-change Jews so that no one would be able to accuse them of prejudice or discrimination.

Application to Marriage

While on the surface it might appear that I have drifted away from discussing marital negotiation, this incident helps us understand how negotiation should go on in marriage. (Later chapters will spell out the specifics of application in great detail.) There was a genuine grievance in which one party felt the situation was unfair, that they were not receiving commensurately with what they were giving. They did not suppress their grievance but were honest and open in expressing it. The other party (Jews) should have responded immediately and negotiated a fair arrangement. Unfortunately, they did not, but at least they were willing to let a third party negotiate a compromise settlement, and they accepted what was proposed. There was mutual submission on both sides.

Presumably, both the Jews and the Hellenists were very

satisfied with the outcome. Neither side may have gotten everything it wanted, but each got enough to make them see the solution as *fair*.

Very often marital compromise is just that way; each partner gets something but not all each originally wanted. But each is satisfied not only with what s/he got, but also and very importantly, because s/he knows that his/her partner is also satisfied with what s/he received. In effect each has made the other "happy."

AN IMPORTANT FAMILY DECISION

Based on this incident from Acts, I would like now to begin to show how love and justice might be connected to an important family decision:

Harold Larkin is a minister of a growing church. He's been there for three years and he sees many more years of "fruitful growth" ahead. Alice has faithfully encouraged Harold for the six years of their marriage—during seminary and at his church. She has shown him great love, and he is well aware of it. Alice now feels God wants her to go to seminary and earn a theological degree. Their denominational seminary is in another city. They had lived there for the first three years of their marriage, during which time she had worked as a secretary to pay family bills, including Harold's tuition and books. Now she approaches Harold in terms of both love and justice because the two themes actually are inseparable. She communicates very openly to him that out of *love* for her, he ought to resign his church and move back with her and try to find another church close to the seminary. In this way, Alice says, "You will be showing the kind of love and support the Bible encourages and that I have always shown for you." She builds a natural bridge to the justice question: "Since I have done so much for you, isn't it only right and fair that you do *at least* as much for me? Shouldn't you in response at least go the *first mile?*"

Harold may respond by saying that out of *love* for him she should not ask him to leave his present church. "Too much is happening," he says. "It isn't fair or right to ask me to leave just now." Harold too uses arguments based on both love and justice. Both he and Alice have made perfectly reasonable and "spiritual" arguments.

But who should sacrifice *most* (or love most) at this particular point in time? Who should show the greater love through the greater sacrifice? Should Alice *love* by staying where she is? Should she sacrifice going to seminary so Harold can continue his work? Or should he show greater love by sacrificing his work so she can go into the ministry? What is fair? Where does mutual submission enter in?

I'm not going to suggest how such a situation could be negotiated until chapter 3. The point here is that it is oversimplification of the worst sort merely to say, "Let love have its way"; "Love and all will be well"; "If we love we don't have to worry about justice." There is the possibility for love on *both* sides for the Larkins. Each can outdo the other in love. Simultaneously, each can outdo the other in the generosity with which they bargain—as Abraham did with Lot. Is it possible for one of them to hurt the other by being too generous? Who should bend the most so as to be the most fair toward the other? The kinds of complex, yet burning questions raised in this issue simply cannot be answered by a hierarchical view of male leadership. Indeed, they are never even brought up, because from that perspective they are irrelevant. Yet those are precisely the kinds of issues that Christianity is all about.

From the hierarchical "male leadership" viewpoint, it's acceptable for Harold to try to *impose* a solution on their dilemma. However, recall from Acts 6 that even the Apostles didn't try to *impose* any solution on the church. They did not say, "God has appointed us head over you and you must obey us; we have to have the final decision." In the first place, there were twelve of them. No one Apostle had any final say; they acted as a committee, unlike those who argue that a family has to have *one* final authority. Second, what they did was *communicate* their feelings of injustice at having to serve food. They didn't pull rank and simply say, "We *won't* do it." Rather, they said, "Don't you see, it doesn't make sense for you people to insist on our doing this." They were conciliatory and humble at the same time that they were frank and candid. Had the Jews or Hellenists come up with a better or more fair solution than their own, they would in all likelihood have been willing to negotiate further— a little of the people's plan, a little of theirs; a little submission on one side, a little on the other.

An Example of Unfortunate Conflict

That's what negotiation is all about—between spouses, parents and children, friends, pastor and people, and in any other situation. Recall the sad happenings in Acts 15 when neither Paul nor Barnabas was willing to compromise. In their first missionary journey they had an assistant (13: 5) named John Mark. After a time, Mark must have thought the going got too rough because he turned around and went home (13: 13). As Paul and Barnabas prepared for their second journey, Barnabas (called "the son of encouragement" in 4: 36) apparently felt Mark had matured over the years and should accompany them once more (15: 37). But Paul disagreed; he "thought best not to take with them one who had withdrawn from them . . . and had not gone with them to the work" (15: 38).

Who was right? Paul, who felt that past unfaithfulness and unreliability would be repeated; or Barnabas, who felt that Mark was a changed man and deserved a second chance? What would have been most fair for Mark? For Paul and Barnabas?

It turns out that they could not compromise: "There arose a sharp contention, so that they separated from each other" (v. 39). Barnabas and Mark went in one direction while Paul and Silas went in another. Apparently the church sided with Paul because they "commended" him to God's grace, but there's no record of their doing that for Barnabas. (Unfortunately, we all know too many present-day churches that have split because neither side discovered any compromise they could live with.) Shouldn't there have been one final authority? Shouldn't Barnabas have deferred to Paul, who was clearly the more prestigeful leader throughout the churches?

Or, should Paul have compromised in some way? After all, surely God forgave Mark and showed mercy to him; why couldn't Paul? As a matter of fact, many years later Paul probably wondered the same thing. In 2 Timothy 4: 11 he acknowledges that John Mark is a highly valued Christian worker, and he wants Mark near him while he's in prison. What if Barnabas had spurned Mark the way Paul did? Would Mark have turned out to be as valuable to Paul as he actually later became? Not likely. Nor is it likely that Mark would have written the account of Jesus' life on which Matthew and Luke are apparently based. In other words, Barnabas's arguments back in Acts 15 that Paul should take mercy on Mark were evidently correct. But when Paul was unwilling to negotiate the matter, he destroyed both a deep friendship and an effective partnership in God's service. How much Paul must in later years have regretted that stubborn decision!

What this incident clearly illustrates is that any of us can be wrong about any decision at any time. We must approach negotiations and decisions with a spirit of humility and awareness of our fallibility. This applies in particular to male/female negotiations, where in the past, men have often adopted a posture similar to Paul's. They have thought of themselves as the final arbiter of family decisions, but they have seldom thought about the serious consequences of what happens when they are wrong. Christian women seldom had the financial independence or personal courage to "stand up" to their husbands as Barnabas did to Paul. Today, however, many of them are doing just that, and because husbands are unable or unwilling to compromise, or because neither partner negotiates very well, many separate or divorce. They split in the same way as Paul and Barnabas. In many cases, that splitting can be avoided. What it takes is a *spirit* to negotiate, a willingness to submit to one another, and continual development of practical negotiating skills. It is to those and related matters that we will turn in the next chapter.

3.
APPROACHING
MARITAL CONFLICT

FRED SERVED for several years as a staff worker for a Christian campus organization. Then he and his wife, Cheryl, arrived at a decision: he would resign his position and stay at home to give full-time attention to their three small children. She had just gotten a fellowship to pursue her doctoral studies, and that would be enough to support their family. Their lives were completely altered because of this major decision, and the consequences were bound to be felt for years to come.

Some types of decisions are not over such profound matters. They cover mundane matters such as how to install toilet paper rolls—should they feed from the bottom or the top? Should the car's dome light be allowed to come on during the daylight when the car door is opened, or should it be kept off in daylight?

Sandy writes that on both of these as well as other "little contests of wills" she was engaged in a "cold war" with her husband.[1] Bill wanted the toilet paper and the dome light and several other trivia one way, while she wanted them done another way. Her idea of a "happy marriage" was one where there was "rarely an argument, never a fight, mutual enjoyment. . . ."

So she arrived at a decision to stop dueling with her husband over these "minor" things: "I've given in to Bill's preferences on every single one." How did she decide that?

Or take something in between the profound and the mundane. Marie likes to visit her parents on Sundays while George prefers to stay home and putter around the house or else go fishing. She'd like him to go with her, and he'd like her to stay with him. Complicating the matter are their children and church attendance. Marie wants the children with her so they can attend a Sunday school near her parents' home. George would like the kids to be with him in "the great outdoors"— especially since he doesn't see them all week because of his job as a traveling salesman. What to do?

People who adhere to some form of traditional marital hierarchy would tell Marie to "submit cheerfully, immediately and without reservation to all her husband's wishes because it is a direct command of God in the Bible. She should obey even though the husband's wishes seem sinful to her."[2] So that's simple: no matter if Marie thinks it's wrong to keep her children from Sunday school—just let George decide and Marie obey.

Chapters 1 and 2 have already examined the idea of marital hierarchy or male headship. The conclusion was that for many reasons "letting George decide" is really no answer at all. In the first place, George might be wrong. But the hierarchy viewpoint has a response for that too: "She is to obey her husband as if he were God himself. She can be as certain of God's will, when her husband speaks, as if God had spoken audibly from heaven. . . . A woman who gives up her will to her husband also relinquishes responsibility for the actions she takes. . . . So if a sin is involved, guilt for the woman's action falls on the husband and not on the wife. . . . In the Bible God consistently rewards wives who obey and punishes those who don't. . . ."[3]

Those who take such an extreme position overlook the story

of Sapphira in Acts 5. Her husband, Ananias, lied to the Apostles about how much money he'd gotten for a land sale, and he was promptly struck dead. Not knowing his fate, Sapphira later also lied. Then Peter says to her, "Why did you *agree together* [to lie]?" (v. 9). Sapphira was an obedient wife who went along with what her husband wanted to do, but that unfortunately got her the same fate as her husband.

I'm not suggesting that any such ominous fate awaits today's women who conform to their husband's wishes and whims without any negotiation. But other negative things can happen, some of which we've already considered in earlier chapters. The basic point is: how can couples like George and Marie agree together (to use Peter's phrase) on a course of action that is best for all parties concerned? Incidentally, it's not too hard to figure out how Bill and Sandy arrived at their decision. They apparently share the view that "God, Christ, man and woman are lined up in the universe in that order." [4]

A Passion for Justice

At the end of chapter 2 we left Harold and Alice in limbo. Alice was wanting to go to seminary so that she could join the growing numbers of American women who are becoming ordained ministers.

Before we go on to examine any further steps in their negotiation, let us look at an important facet of the problem they are facing. There are some Christians who believe that Alice and Harold could be spared a lot of grief if she just gave up her idea of being a minister. "Ordination is for men only," they say. There are many arguments for and against women's ordination, and I happen to accept the ones in favor of it. But I have also become convinced that the matter goes much farther than merely rational arguments. Beyond purely *intellectual* appeals to Scripture, theology, church history, and so forth, lies something else, and it is at the core of the Bible, namely, the passion for justice.

I was struck by this "something else" as I read a *New York Times* account of the first married couple ever ordained together into the Episcopal priesthood. Their vows were administered by the Bishop of Massachusetts, who also happens to be the man's father. "In a resounding voice, his face glistening with tears, Bishop Coburn asked the couple before him: 'My Sister and Brother, do you believe that you are truly called by God and His church to the priesthood?' 'I believe I am so called.'"[5] The article goes on to describe the rest of the ceremony. When it was over, the congregation broke into spontaneous applause. The rector of the church rose and asked his congregation, "Is there a dry eye in the house?" People were weeping and greeting each with hugs, the modern version of the "holy kiss" talked about in the New Testament.

Why was there weeping at a joyous occasion like that? Other women have been ordained as ministers or priests and the feelings have not run that deeply, nor have those ordinations been reported in such detail by a national newspaper. The uniqueness of this event was that a husband and wife were taking their sacred vows simultaneously. The event symbolized their intent to be genuine *co*-workers in God's service. It also symbolizes that *in no way* can this particular woman be thought of as subordinate or secondary to her husband. They are truly interchangeable in their work roles as well as in their domestic roles.

I believe it was precisely the fact that a married woman had attained that status with her husband that stirred the hearts of the congregation. The event symbolized a significant milestone on the long journey upward towards justice for women. That sense that justice was being done, that atonement was being made for the wrongs and injustices to women of previous centuries—that is what gripped the hearts and minds of the congregation that day. Many Christians have become convinced that it is right for women to be ordained; and to actually see it happen in that unique way stirs the soul in a way that no logical arguments are able to do.

What does that sort of soul-stirring have to do with marital negotiation and conflict? Simply this—the foundation that underlies effective negotiation and mutual submission is that same kind of passion for justice, concern that others be treated fairly and equitably. That passion should stir with particular force if the others have been underdogs, if they have been treated unjustly and unfairly in the past: for example, Chicanos, blacks, poor whites, women.

Thus as far as marital negotiation is concerned, men have a special responsibility to cultivate that passion, that feeling for justice, for what is right and fair. But by the same token, women must cultivate it just as strongly. Relying purely on men's goodwill fails to take into account the fact that frail human beings are either knowingly or unknowingly selfish, and must be checked.

Cultivating Justice

If this sense of justice (and outrage at injustice) is the starting point for marital negotiations, how does one cultivate it? It is to be hoped that our parents began to instill it into us by precept and example. But whether that happened or not, there is always room to hone the sense of justice and fair play ever more keenly. "Iron sharpens iron, and one man sharpens another" (Prov. 27: 17, RSV). The best way to sharpen one's passion for fair play is to have one's spouse call the other up short if s/he isn't fair. In other words, each acts like iron, showing the other where s/he is being unfair, or selfish.

Many women have great difficulty being that sort of sharpener, or iron. Young girls are trained at home, church, and school to act more like butter in the face of male demands.

Women must consciously face this lack of honing ability and seek to develop it. Another commonly used term for the same quality is assertiveness, and there are several good books available to help women enhance their assertiveness.[6] Those books will also help men to help women be more assertive.

But suppose a woman *is* assertive? Suppose she tells her husband he is being unfair—his passion for justice is awry. What then?

HAROLD AND ALICE

Let's go back to Harold and Alice. As I described it in chapter 2, both of them are engaging in what I call *explicit* negotiation. That is, each one is *openly,* freely, and consciously presenting his/her side. If you reread pages 47–48, you will see that Alice is using a negotiating strategy called "moral obligation." She is saying, "I have done so much for you in the past that now you owe me something. You ought to reciprocate."

Negotiating Techniques

Harold is using a bargaining strategy called "individual well-being." He is saying, "Look, for *my sake* we can't leave now." It is quite possible for them to continue indefinitely negotiating with each other in just those ways. In many marriages some disagreements are never resolved or "made to go away," because one or both partners is/are content to have the disagreement continue for a long period of time. And if at least one partner is not concerned about how long it's taking to resolve the matter, it could persist indefinitely. We will look at those kinds of conflicts in later chapters.

The Import of Time

Time, in other words, is a crucial element in all negotiations. If it doesn't matter *when* a disagreement is resolved, does it really matter at all? If Alice didn't care *when* she enrolled in seminary, how important is it to her? But to Alice it does matter *when,* because she wants to start some sort of pastoral ministry as soon as possible. Remember that for six years she has been supportive of her husband's ministry. Now it's time, she thinks, for a change.

Compromise

Therefore, she's been trying to get him to change his behavior and move with her by using her "obligation" strategy, but so far he hasn't been willing. Instead, he's been countering her strategy with his strategy. So now she adds something to the negotiations—the element of a compromise offer. She had originally said: "Let's move this coming summer." Now she is willing to wait, so she says to him, "Would you move a year from this summer?"

Fair Play

Now at that point a sense of fair play, or the rules of fair bargaining or "bargaining in good faith," require him to make some sort of meaningful response. He's not supposed to ignore her suggestion, although he can. But one acid test of a person's passion for justice and mutual submission is his/her willingness to respond in a meaningful way to any serious suggestion or offer made by the spouse. If Harold merely ignores what Alice has said, then he's really not concerned for fair play.

Responding doesn't necessarily mean the next minute.

Harold said, "Give me a few days to pray and think about it." But notice the time element again. Alice considers a few days perfectly fair. But if Harold says three months, or if he refuses to set any limits at all on how much time he needs, Alice will feel that he is simply putting her off. And she'll be no better off than before she made her compromise offer—the disagreement could continue to go on indefinitely.

After a few days, Harold responds by *rejecting* her compromise. He explains that after praying and thinking, he can't leave. He says he believes God wants him to stay where he is. It would be too costly to his ministry, he says, and costly to his career as a minister to leave, even next year. So in effect, she must bear the cost of not achieving what she believes God wants her to do, whereas he's not bearing any costs at all in this matter.

Power

Incidentally, we've just seen *power* at work. Some people say power is a nasty word, that power doesn't belong in a love relationship. The fact is that, whether we like it or not, power is as unavoidable as the weather. It shadows all human relationships at all times, even when it's equally apportioned, which isn't often. In the situation above, however, it's clearly not equal. Power can be defined in many ways, but one defintion is the capability to achieve goals at the lowest possible cost.

By that definition it's easy to see that right now Harold is exercising more power than Alice over the situation. What's happening is very costly to her, but so far not costly at all to Harold.

Another rule of fair play is that when one party rejects an offer, as Harold did, *he/she* is obligated to come up with some kind of counter-offer. It's not enough to reject it and forget it; that's not being fair to Alice. That's not taking her negotiations seriously. Harold, like many men before him, would be showing that he didn't have much of a passion for women's justice, and little genuine interest in mutual submission. Men have had great difficulty in taking women seriously when they step out of traditional roles. Many men just can't believe that a woman scientist, astronaut, athlete, president, boss is for real. And a woman who wants to be a minister and who expects her husband to make sacrifices (pay certain costs, and not just financial ones)—that's just too much for a lot of men to accept.

Harold's Offer

In later chapters we'll examine what happens when men react to women that way, but for the time being, Harold is not like that. He does want to try to play fair; and so he makes what he considers to be a reasonable counter-offer. While in college Alice didn't take certain language courses which are required before she can take actual seminary courses. To help students get ready for seminary, the school offers these prerequisites by mail. So Harold says, "Why don't you enroll in the courses that our seminary offers by mail? That way you could start working toward your seminary degree, and in a couple of years we'll see if you still want to go to the seminary, and if I'm ready to move."

In this potential compromise, there is some cost to Harold, if only financial. He says the money for the correspondence courses would come out of his salary. How should Alice respond? She could give up the matter entirely and say that since she doesn't like to take courses by mail she'll just forget her seminary goals altogether. Or she could accept his offer, or she could reject it as is. If she does reject it, then in order to play fair with Harold she has to come up with a counter-offer, or at least a meaningful response. After all, he is taking her seriously enough to negotiate with her.

But is he taking her seriously? What if he is just trying to "take her for a ride"? People can bargain with different objectives in mind. Some bargain only to enhance their own profit or well-being. The salesperson who travels door to door may be doing this. You've never seen him/her before, and since *he/she* never expects to deal with you again (unlike your local dealer), you the customer may be victimized or exploited.

Another objective is to bargain solely for the good of the other, as many women have traditionally dealt with men. The basic problem with that approach is that it makes the recipient greedy and selfish. Both the one doing all the giving and the one doing all the receiving end up suffering.

Maximum Joint Profit

The best objective in bargaining is to aim for what has been called maximum *joint* profit, or MJP. Closely tied to justice, MJP is the essence of what Paul meant by "mutual submission." What could be fairer than all parties concerned receiving as many benefits as they possibly can? Furthermore, if all parties are benefiting that much, they're not likely to want to leave the relationship, so it's likely to last for a long time. Our door-to-door salesman is precisely the opposite. His/her goal is maximum *individual* profit, MIP.

In marriage, as in most other relationships, each partner usually has some idea of whether their spouse deals with them in terms of MJP, MIP, or somewhere in between. "Does he/she really care about my interests, my goals, my needs, my desires, my feelings; or does he/she think most or even solely of his/her own well-being?

That's the deeper question Alice is asking herself as she ponders whether Harold is trying to take her for a ride. "Is the correspondence study merely a gimmick to put me off? Does he really want me to develop my God-given gifts to their fullest capacity? Or is he chiefly concerned about his pastorate, with my wishes being merely incidental?" In the early stages of discussion or negotiation over a matter, it's not always a simple matter to detect whether one's partner is motivated by MJP or MIP bargaining goals. Of course, if you've known and lived with that person for some time, you have a pretty good idea about their overall bargaining objectives. Some people are consistently MJP, others consistently MIP; many go back and forth between the two.

For instance, a person like Harold, who has always been extremely MJP toward Alice, can nonetheless shift. What often brings about a shift like that is the gravity of the particular issue. Up to now Harold and Alice have never disagreed over anything quite as important as this is to both of them. The fact is, however, that pastors and marriage counselors around the country seem to be reporting an upsurge in just these sorts of grave matters. As long as Christian women were content to be subservient to their husbands, and felt no particular calling to serve God with all their talents in the same ways that men do, the chances for grave marital conflicts were much smaller than now. Today, an increasing number of Christian women *of all ages* are no longer content with being stifled or suffocated, any more than men are.

Conflict As Healthy

Therefore, conflicts of all sorts are bound to be more frequent. That is no cause for hand-wringing, however. Instead these new situations provide formerly unknown opportunities to develop creative solutions. Conflict per se is not a sign of ill health. Quite the contrary! It can be a sure indication of health, vigor, and vitality!

Alice cares enough about their relationship to press her case. To suppress her desires would be emotionally and spiritually unhealthy. To ignore or forget them would be equally unhealthy. But because she cares about Harold and about their marriage she wants to try to resolve their disagreement. In short, conflict can be a very healthy thing for marriage, first, because it brings grievances out into the open, instead of letting them simmer beneath the surface. Second, conflict is positive because the process of negotiation, of resolving the conflict through mutual submission, can bind the couple together more strongly than before they began to bargain.

This theme of marital negotiation and conflict as a positive force in marriage runs through this entire chapter and indeed the entire book. It underlies everything we're saying. But right now let's return to Alice as she ponders what kind of response she should make to Harold, and whether or not he genuinely has her best interests at heart, whether his bargaining objectives are actually based on MJP or not.

Alice's Promise

First of all, Alice rejects Harold's offer of correspondence study because she says she needs personal contacts with teachers and students. Next she shifts her bargaining strategy from trying to get him to see his "moral obligation" (which hasn't worked) to another kind of strategy—promises. In passing, let me comment that sometimes a "moral obligation" strategy does "work"; it does bring a disagreement to a satisfactory resolution. What one needs to do is to sense when such a strategy might be appropriate to use. If you think it might be effective, go ahead and try it. If it doesn't accomplish much, don't be discouraged. Be flexible and try a different strategy, as Alice does.

Alice says to Harold, "If you will agree to move a year from summer (her earlier compromise offer), then I will do something you've always wanted me to do but which I have never done. I will become active in the women's groups of our church; I'll try to set the example for them that you want."

Duty

But he rejects that strategy with another type of bargaining strategy, namely, an appeal to *duty*. You can negotiate with others by saying they should do something because it is part of their role. "If you're a student, you *should* study"; "If you're an employer you should pay your workers"; and so on. Harold tells Alice, "If you're a minister's wife, you should be active in the church's women's groups—it's your duty."

Most couples, as I said before, have areas of disagreement that are never completely resolved—that just persist indefinitely. In this case Alice has, in the past, rejected the strategy that such activity is her duty; and most of the time, Harold never tries to negotiate her into changing. He simply lets the matter lie dormant. This time Alice has brought it up in the context of a promise, but also as a major *compromise* on her part.

But Harold fails to see just how much of a concession she is willing to make. He doesn't see it as a compromise at all, but as something she *should* do anyway. So Alice explains that the reason she doesn't like to be involved in the women's groups is that they don't understand or agree with her desire to be an autonomous person in general, and a minister in particular. They put pressure on her to behave in a more "traditional" fashion, and look askance at her ideas to have study groups examining changes in men's and women's roles. "Nevertheless," says Alice to Harold, "I will take part in those groups at great personal cost to myself (autonomy) if you will agree to a move a year from now."

But in spite of two major compromises on her part (the time factor and the women's groups) Harold refuses to agree to that move. Suddenly, Alice begins to doubt his concern for MJP. She begins to feel that he is primarily concerned for his own well-being and is not fulfilling Paul's words in Philippians 2: 4: "Let each of you look not only to his own interests, but also to the interests of others." It begins to occur to her that Harold may not actually be interested in mutual submission after all.

By not being moved by the enormity (from Alice's standpoint) of her concession in being willing to work with the women's groups, Harold has not only missed the opportunity to resolve the matter fairly quickly, but he has contributed to its escalation. In some respects negotiation is like driving a freeway. There are critical junctures (exits) that can take you with equal speed to or from your goal. The importance of being alert for and taking the right freeway exit is well known to any driver!

Escalation

Negotiation is often like that. There are critical points at which the alert negotiator can take steps to resolve a disagreement or deescalate a conflict. If those exits are missed, the result is usually sharper conflict. That happened here. Harold "missed his exit," and the fact that Alice doubts his MJP motivation means their conflict is probably now going to be escalated. It's going to get sharper and probably hotter.

4.

BUILDING MARITAL ACCORDS

Alice's Well-Being

Before Alice escalates her conflict with Harold in earnest, she will try one more persuasion-type bargaining strategy. Moral-obligation strategy didn't work; neither did promise. Now she tries an appeal (that Harold used earlier) based on her own individual self-interest or well-being. She asks Harold to agree because it would be best for her if he did so! She explains that she feels very strongly that God wants her in seminary; that otherwise her talents will be wasted, she will feel empty and unfulfilled, and she will indeed fail to receive the kinds of eternal rewards about which we talked in chapter 2.

At first, some people might object to using one's own well-being as a legitimate negotiating strategy. But, as pointed out in chapter 2, concern for one's own well-being is not censured by Jesus or Paul. Jesus tells us to love our neighbor as ourself. Instead, it is *selfish* concern that excludes other's interests that is wrong, as Philippians 2:4 (above) indicates. In contrast it is merely *false* humility that is fearful of communicating a self-interest strategy. Alice's past, present, and promised future behaviors hardly indicate she's selfish; quite the contrary, she wants what's best for *both* her husband and herself. She has already been practicing mutual submission; she merely wants Harold to do the same.

Labeling

But Harold rejects this strategy also. He again fails to be sensitive to her deepest concerns; he once more misses an opportunity to resolve the matter. So Alice escalates by putting a name on—labeling—his behavior. She tells him he is being selfish—that he is concerned only for his own well-being (MIP) not hers. In doing that she is actually doing him a favor. She is fulfilling every Christian's responsibility to be a *Nathan* (see chap. 2, p. 31). In the past women have hesitated to be Nathans (or "iron," as described earlier), and men, women, and marriage have suffered accordingly.

Anger and Withdrawal

When you label someone's behavior in a negative way like that ("you're being selfish") you run a risk, of course. The hope is that this tactic will shock the other person into change (as it did King David) or (in Harold's case) into bargaining for an acceptable compromise. But it can also make the other person angry. Their anger could cause them to withdraw from any active bargaining at all. That's not keeping to the rules of fair play, but some persons do it anyhow. It is, in fact, its own strategy. If Harold should "clam up," become distant and say, "I don't want to discuss it any more," he is in fact trying to preserve things as they are. Interestingly, research evidence shows that men tend to use this withdrawal technique more often than women. And sometimes, because they don't know how to respond to it, women tend to be "thrown" by this sort of strategy and simply give up their goals.

But withdrawal won't resolve this issue, because Alice won't give up. So the risk she runs by pointing out his selfishness is facing Harold's anger. He may become angry and hostile toward her, raise his voice, turn purple and shout that *she* is the one who is being selfish! She shouldn't want to go to seminary and have him leave his church!

Some people feel that anger is unhealthy; a few even think it's sinful. In reality the issue is not that simple. How anger is to be judged depends on the *cause* and the *consequences* of the anger. In the Old Testament the prophets often became angry at injustice (as did King David). Jesus became angry at the misuse of the Temple by conniving merchants. Both Jesus and the prophets had good cause to be angry—injustice and wrong-doing. The prophets' anger resulted in denunciation of the kings and priests—a worthy outcome. Jesus physically ejected the offending parties from the Temple. Throwing them out was also a worthy outcome, and resulted in no bodily harm to the merchants.

Violence

The anger demonstrated in the preceding examples has been called "right" or "justifiable" anger. However, violence that results from failure to control our anger is wrong and damaging. In recent years all of us have become increasingly aware of the great amount of violence that goes on in families. Sociologists have found that, next to the police, the family is our most violent social institution! Men beat and abuse their wives and children. Women have also been guilty of beating and abusing their children, and in some cases their husbands as well. Fathers, mothers, and older children use guns and knives on one another. These are terribly undesirable outcomes of anger, and unfortunately they all too often occur in Christian families.

Many students of family violence are convinced (and I concur) that a great deal of it can be attributed to the hierarchical views of marriage described earlier. The imagery of hammers, chisels, anvils bespeak macho strength and set the stage for possible violence. We would go a long way toward reducing family violence by emphasizing the equality of the sexes in all matters, including decision-making. The more boys and men develop a healthy respect for women as qualified decision-makers, the less likely they are to strike out at them.

Harold respects Alice. He knows she is spiritually devout, intelligent, and kind. He knows that she has contributed much to him. For him to get violent with her would be totally out of place, as well as morally wrong. But he is angry, and controlled anger (anger that avoids violence) can be a bargaining strategy. It gives the other party an indication of how strongly you feel about something. Harold feels that Alice's goals are so unjust and unfair that they make him terribly angry.

Alice, of course, feels just as strongly that his ideas are unfair, and she could become angry too. They could shout at each other and call each other lots of names. Let's assume they do just that. But when their mutual anger has all been vented, the problem's still not resolved. They may have had an exercise in emotional therapy, but now what?

Deescalation

What happens is that Alice sees the need to deescalate. Harold's anger has revealed to her a depth of feeling of which she had previously been unaware. She had not known how unfair he thinks she is. Since he has not come up with a creative resolution she will have to do so—a very creative solution that somehow will permit him to remain in his present church while at the same time permitting her to attend seminary. God has made some people more creative than the rest of us. But all of us can train ourselves to be more creative than we are. One of the ways to do that is never to exclude any idea, no matter how absurd or weird or "far out" others may think it is.

As Alice seeks for a creative resolution, she is aware that in the past it has been very common for men to be away from their wives and children for days, weeks, months—occasionally even years at a time—in order to work or to go to school. Traveling salesmen try to come home on weekends, although they can't always do it. Military men are often away for protracted periods of time. And while busy politicians, pastors, businessmen, storekeepers, and others may make it to their own bed every night, they often don't get there until midnight or after, and are gone again at 6:00 or 7:00 A.M. Nobody objected to that behavior in principle, except to warn men that they might be neglecting their wives and children.

Alice is also aware that a small but increasing number of married couples are apart during the week but commute on weekends. For instance, the editorial page editor of the *New York Times* works in New York, while her surgeon husband works in Cleveland.[1] On weekends one partner travels to be with the other. I know of a situation in which the husband is graduate student at a university some eighty miles from where his wife is a minister. He spends the week at the university and the weekends at home, having entered that arrangement after spending several years at another parish where they were co-ministers. Therefore, since men have often left their families for weeks and months at a time in order to pursue their vocation (e.g., missionaries, pastors, merchants, seamen, soldiers, construction workers), all that is happening now is that women feel they should have the same privilege that men have always had.

Creative Resolution

Given these trends, Alice develops a creative resolution to their disagreement. She believes it's "an offer he can't refuse" because it's fair to both of them. It is based on mutual submission. It achieves what they *both* most want—he to stay at his church; she to go to seminary. Very simply, she indicates to him that this coming fall (not the following fall, as would have been the case had he been willing to go with her) she will go to the seminary during the week and commute home on the weekends. From her savings and with loans she will even pay for her own tuition and living expenses!

Given this bargain, Harold can't accuse Alice of being selfish in wanting him to leave his church. In fact there isn't much that he can do besides agree to it. Earlier I had suggested that Harold was demonstrating more power than Alice by rejecting her compromise offer regarding a move. But now their power has become fairly equalized.

Harold controlled the situation as long as Alice thought that she needed him with her in order to accomplish her goal of moving. But as soon as she and he both realized that she was not dependent on him in that particular way, his control diminished. She was free to go. Dependency is an important part of power. To depend on someone is to grant them power over you. That's not undesirable as long as the dependence is not one way—as long as both parties depend on each other.

In Alice and Harold's case, their dependence on one another has now become fairly equal. However, in many (probably most) marriages, the woman is more dependent on the man than the other way around. The woman tends to be more dependent because the husband earns most, if not all, the family income. In contrast, Alice earns enough money to support herself through seminary. Perhaps even more important, many women are also more dependent because they often lack the courage and assertiveness to negotiate as Alice has, and many lack the courage to ask their husbands to pay the price Harold will have to pay. They also lack the determination to pay that kind of price themselves.

Mutual Submission Is Not Free

What price do I mean? Both Alice and Harold have gotten what they wanted, but each has also had to give up the other's companionship, colleagueship, mutual support, and so on, during the week. Each was willing for the price of mutual submission, but relatively few women would ask their husbands to pay it so that they could develop their talents as Alice wants to do. Moreover, relatively few women would see the benefits they would receive (e.g., schooling, or an occupation) as worth the price.

When I say "relatively few" I mean, compared to men. More men than women would ask their spouses to pay that sort of price, and more men than women would see those benefits as worthwhile. Nevertheless, there are more women today than ten years ago for whom both things would apply. What is more, there will be more women ten years from now than today for whom both things will be true.

Another price both Alice and Harold will have to pay is the gossip of the church members. Many of them will surely be critical of Alice for going off during the week, and critical of Harold for "letting" her.

It is through no fault of their own, however, that women have been hesitant to pay and ask for these various costs. Prior chapters have pointed out that women learn from their earliest days that their main mission in life is to serve men. That would be fine, but men have not learned that they are equally obligated to serve women. For the most part, women are still ending up being unfairly taken advantage of.

There is no reason why Harold can't serve Alice in this way, no reason he can't sacrifice, and pay these costs. Indeed, as strange as it may sound, he should be happy to do it, because *it means so much to her*. It will make her so happy. Out of love for her he ought to say, with Jacob, who became Laban's indentured servant for seven years before he could marry Laban's daughter Rachel, that the years "seemed to him but a few days [for Harold, in other words, it should seem almost nothing] because of the love he had for her" (Gen. 29:20).

There is every reason for Alice to want to pay the costs required by the solution she proposed, because it will benefit her so much in the long run. Thus, in learning how to negotiate creatively with one's spouse, some of the most important lessons a woman (and man) can learn are right in front of us. First, the woman needs to learn to be willing to have her husband pay a certain price—in other words, *sacrifice*—so that her own well-being can be served. Second and, simultaneously, men must learn to be willing to pay such costs—in short, be prepared for mutual submission. Third, women must learn to be willing to forego certain kinds of immediate enjoyments in order to gain benefits that women have not generally had. In other words, while many men have been willing to sacrifice time with, warmth from, and other rewards supplied by wife and children in order to advance their own careers, or to serve God, women have been quite reluctant to do that. Women have also been unwilling to do nontraditional things for fear of the disapproval of friends and relatives. Women need to develop that kind of willingness in a context of creative bargaining so that a balance between outside interests and family is achieved. (Men, of course, need to develop a similar balance.) For example, in the case of Alice and Harold's arrangement, each sees their interpersonal costs as temporary (a few years). Furthermore, the costs are experienced only for periods of a few days at a time.

Steps to Consensus

At this point we can put a label on the compromise agreement to which Alice and Harold have come in this and the prior chapter. We can say that they have reached a *consensus* based on *explicit* bargaining. Being explicit means that each person has fully and verbally communicated his/her intentions and feelings. Everything has been "up front"; there has been little if any subtle or nonverbal, or *implicit*, bargaining—a topic to which we will return below.

Let's briefly outline the points by which Alice and Harold got to this consensus. Then when you're trying to arrive at an agreement with your spouse, you will have a guide to some of the principles to use and follow. Keep in mind there are more principles still to be discussed, but these provide a start. Remember also that by showing how Harold and Alice arrived at a fair agreement, I have presented numerous strategies that married couples can apply to *any* disagreement they have. In connection with the principles of chapters 1 and 2, these can go a long way towards helping couples resolve disagreements and conflicts.

1. Alice saw that she had to be an *iron sharpener*.

2. She first used a bargaining strategy called *moral obligation*.

3. Harold then reacted with a bargaining strategy called *individual well-being*.

4. Alice was aware of the crucial import of the time dimension.

5. She is willing to make compromises.

6. Both are generally sensitive to, and follow *rules of fair play*, or *bargaining in good faith*.

7. Harold shows power by rejecting all her compromises in which she is *dependent* on him, that is, in which he must agree to move before she will.

8. To show he takes Alice's intentions seriously, Harold offers compromises of his own.

9. Both in general are bargaining with *maximum joint profit* (MJP) as a goal.

9.1. Neither Harold nor Alice are afraid of marital conflict.

They recognize it to be a healthy and positive thing.

10. Alice switches her bargaining strategy, this time using a strategy of *promise*, tied to a very major compromise.

11. He rejects that offer, and responds with a *duty* strategy.

11.1. Harold has missed an opportunity to deescalate the conflict, and Alice begins to doubt his concern for MJP.

12. She switches strategies again, this time using *self-interest*, or *well-being*, as Harold had done before (cf. no. 3).

13. Harold again misses a chance to deescalate.

14. Alice escalates by labeling his behavior as selfish, as *maximum individual profit* (MIP).

14.1. She thus runs the risk of his withdrawal or his anger.

15. He reacts with anger, which provides Alice with new insight.

15.1. She feels they need to deescalate.

16. She makes a creative compromise he can't refuse.

16.1. It achieves what they both want.

16.2. She is not dependent on him to carry it out.

16.3. It entails costs for both of them.

16.4. He considers it fair, nevertheless, and they have finally arrived at consensus.

As you study these points and reflect on the full story from which they are drawn, note several things. First, both partners kept on talking, discussing, "communicating," the entire time. Neither one withdrew into a shell and refused to negotiate. Nor did Harold do what many men have told me they do—pontificate: "I am the head of this household. Since we cannot arrive at an agreement, God has given me the responsibility to decide." Alice was eminently flexible and creative in her bargaining strategies. She never became discouraged or gave up. If one strategy couldn't get Harold to change (no. 2), she moved to another (no. 10), then another (no. 12).

At the same time that Alice was trying to get Harold to change, she herself was changing, making important compromises (nos. 5, 10, 16). He too made some compromises (no. 8), but overall he wasn't willing to change his behavior as much as she wanted him to, or as much as she was willing to change her own. Alice sensed this and confronted him with it. That made him angry. And even though Alice also became angry, Harold was insensitive to how much Alice really wanted her goals, and also insensitive to opportunities to resolve their disagreement.

But Alice was not only flexible; she became, because of his anger, very sensitive to how much Harold actually wanted *his* goal. Therefore, to her array of bargaining skills—flexibility, compromises, sensitivity—is added creativity. She lets her mind range freely to come up with a solution which, though not without its price, they both consider fair and just.

Earlier I said Harold should be commended because he took Alice's negotiations so seriously. Harold should also be commended for something else. He *understood* her need to achieve. He knew that it is just as important to her to be using her gifts and talents as it is to him. And though he tried to delay indefinitely her going to seminary, he was sensitive enough to her to recognize when she finally made an uncontestable offer. Just as Harold's anger had made Alice see something about him she had not seen before, so her willingness to propose this innovative solution brought her aspirations into sharper focus for him. Realizing their overwhelming importance to her, he knew there was no way he could remain opposed. If fair play, justice and equity, and mutual submission have any meaning at all to Harold (and they do) he had to cooperate.

Change and Imagination

Perhaps the main reason that Alice was the more assertive, imaginative, and effective negotiator was that it was she who wanted something new and different. The partner who prefers things as they are thinks about change as little as s/he can. It is the one who wants change who is constantly trying to figure out ways to bring it about.

Right now, for instance, both Alice and Harold have agreed to postpone having children. But suppose in a year or two Harold begins to press Alice to change her behavior and to become pregnant. If she thinks that's not a good idea, then very likely it will be he who will come up with the creative solutions, offer compromises, use effective bargaining strategies, and so forth. And then it will be she who prefers things as they are, thinks about it as little as she can, prefers to put it off, gets angry if he accuses her of being selfish, and so on.

In short, the *situation* one is in is a major influence as to how, if at all, one negotiates with one's partner. Being in a situation of wanting change is vastly different from being in a situation of not wanting change, of preferring the status quo.

Means and Ends

Sometimes, of course, both partners want change, and that can simplify negotiations because they have the same goal. Unlike Alice and Harold, who started their bargaining with different goals, Sue and Tom have the same goal—to buy a new car. If Sue thought they shouldn't, but Tom wanted to, they would first have had to negotiate the matter of goals or ends— should they or shouldn't they buy a new car? One of them of course, has to bring it up first. Tom might say, "You know, I've been thinking we need a new car." Sue immediately agrees so the goal is settled. Now they have to negotiate the means to arrive at that goal.

Incidentally, among many marriages in the past, decisions like buying cars were usually left with the husband. Some husbands would decide whether or not to get a car, and if so, what kind, how expensive, and other factors. They wouldn't even think of discussing it with their wives; they'd simply announce to them what they were doing or what they had done. Other husbands might first do what Tom did, in other words, obtain their wife's agreement before acting. But once they got their wife's agreement, they would never have bothered to negotiate any more details with them—they would just have gone ahead and bought whatever car they wanted.

Husbands acted that way about cars, and wives let them, because it was held that, after all, he was making the money, so why shouldn't he decide how to spend it? Besides that, cars were men's own special "province," in the way that decorating the house belonged mostly to the woman. She would decide how to spend money to make the *inside* of the house look attractive, so as to reflect their status. Simultaneously he would spend it on an *external* status symbol—the car.

Some women still prefer it that way, but a growing number are like Sue. They want to participate actively in all the decisions about the car (brand, color, price, etc.) including signing for its title, its financing, and its insurance. Sue may not work for pay outside the home, but she works hard inside it, and her efforts make it possible for Tom to earn dollars. So it isn't totally his money after all—it's as much hers as his. And if Sue is employed, then she is even more concerned that money she earns be spent in exactly the way she feels it should be.

In any case, couples should be aware of whether they are negotiating goals or means. As couples think about their disagreements, it often clarifies things to ask themselves and each other: "Are we negotiating *goals* (buy a car, move, take or quit a job, have a child), or *means* to arrive at goals?"

Suppose Tom and Sue make this statement: "We both agree we should change churches, but we can't seem to agree on how to go about finding one in which we can both be at home." In this case, their agreement on goals should make it easier to decide on ways to achieve their goals. If they disagreed over whether or not to change churches, that would mean a lot of hard work still lies ahead of them.

Actually, that previous sentence marks the major difference between negotiations over means versus ends. While the same basic negotiation principles apply in either case, it's a matter of how much hard work they face—how long a road they have to travel to resolution. Once they agree on goals, the road is shorter. If both means and ends are in dispute, the road is a lot longer.

Implicit Agreements

Another way that road is shortened is by a couple's capability to deal with matters before they ever become disagreements. Up to this point, we've talked about explicit and overt negotiations. But in some kinds of matters, some couples find that they know what to do, or what is the best decision, through implicit, understood means.

For example, Ira and Fran are talking to their ten-year-old Beth, and Beth lies to them. Ira and Fran glance at each other, and the expression on each face tells the other they both know it's a lie. But a further expression says, "Let's proceed cautiously in handling this." Each transmits that silent message to the other, both agreeing that is the wise thing to do. So both of them begin talking gently with Beth to help her see they know she's lied, and to try to get her to refrain from lying in the future.

Many times parents disagree strongly with each other over how to discipline their children. Then they have to try to settle their differences through explicit negotiation. But Ira and Fran have settled this discipline matter simply by reading each other's faces. It is possible also to reach understanding by reading body movements and similar subtle, nonverbal messages and reactions.

Sometimes the implicitness becomes a little more overt. For example, often a husband or wife will say to their spouse, "I think I will purchase a chair"; or, "I'm going to take a job"; or, "I'm going to spend a week visiting my brother." The spouse may respond with, "Fine"; "Whatever you say"; "No problem"; or else with a yawn, grunt, or look of indifference.

One spouse has made a verbal "offer," a statement of a goal s/he wants. The partner's response has communicated that s/he does not wish to discuss the change, but simply accepts it as is. Or the other might offer a minor modification which the first person accepts immediately. "If you buy a chair, make it a recliner"—"о.к." "If you take a job, you'll have to pay a baby sitter"—"Fine." "Be sure you clean the house before you make your visit to Sam"—"Sure."

Any one of these matters could conceivably generate sharp disagreements that would require the kinds of explicit bargaining talked about earlier in the chapter, and to be examined further in the next chapter. But in each of these three cases both husband and wife happen to think that both the offers and the modifications are fair, so they are willing to live with them.

I'm sure you can think of many other examples of implicit agreements—matters on which husbands and wives can agree very quickly, because they perceive the immediate resolution to be a fair and just one. It is when the proposed offer or solution is seen as unfair by one or both parties that the couple usually shifts into explicit discussions about it—discussions I have called bargaining.

A Matter of Justice

Focus on fairness brings us full circle to the point at which chapter 3 began. I said there that a passion for justice underlies effective marital negotiations. I've heard several men wonder aloud what Paul meant in Ephesians 5:25 when he said husbands are to "love their wives as Christ loved the church." This statement of course means many things that have been discussed elsewhere.[2] But one thing it surely means is that men should seek to cultivate a passion for justice and fair play toward their wives. Men should take their wives' goals, ideas, objectives, and aspirations seriously. They should negotiate with them as honestly and with as much respect as they would with any man. They ought to learn and practice mutual submission.

But unless women are willing to act like "iron sharpening iron," men are not going to be as passionate for justice as they could or should be. Women have as much responsibility to keep men bargaining for justice as men do to keep themselves on that track.

Did Harold have that kind of passion for justice? Probably as much as most men. And was Alice continually alert to make sure that justice was done? Definitely yes—much more so than many women. But it was that combination of Harold's relative concern for justice and Alice's great concern for it that enabled them to resolve a very grave disagreement in their lives.

Unfortunately, not all couples enjoy that optimal combination. Either the woman is less determined to achieve equity than was Alice; or the man may be less concerned for justice than Harold; or perhaps both these things are true. When that happens, mutual submission is difficult, and conflicts are not easily resolved. In fact, they may become very much an ongoing part of the couple's marriage. That reality becomes the theme of the next several chapters.

5.

LIVING WITH DISAGREEMENTS

REMEMBER MARIE and George? We left them in chapter 3, disagreeing over how they and their children should spend Sundays. Marie would like to be with her parents and have the children in a certain Sunday school. George would prefer that Marie and the children stay home with him so they can "do things together." Hierarchy advocates are fond of using situations such as this to reinforce the idea of female submission. They will say that in their church there was a woman like Marie whose husband would never attend. (Let's call this couple Bruce and Kathy.) One day the preacher told Kathy to stop carping at Bruce and just tell him, "Because I am a Christian I will obey you and stay home with you if that's what you want." When she did that, they say, Bruce became flabbergasted at his wife's "meek and submissive spirit." Because she stopped arguing and was such a changed person, he decided to come to church with her to find out what it meant to be a Christian. Then he too became a Christian and now the whole family sits together in the front pew.

No one doubts that things like this sometimes really happen. But for every story like that there are probably two dozen where Bruce doesn't respond at all to Kathy's sacrifice. So Kathy stays home from church and loses the benefits she could have gotten from the hymns, sermon and fellowship. And her children lose them as well. And Bruce never changes. Everybody loses, including Bruce.

Now, if this scenario were replayed with George and Marie, in the short run he would have what he wanted. But what of the long run? Recall that in chapter 2 we saw that persons who give in to their partner's selfish and unfair demands do them no favor. They actually hurt them by their failure to be "iron sharpening iron."

Indeed, a strong argument can be made that if Marie would try to negotiate a fair compromise with George, George might be impressed with how much Christ meant to her. He might be more willing to explore something for which she stood up than something she merely sat on. Most historians, for instance, concur that the more the early Christians were willing to suffer and die for their faith, the more the officials and citizens of the Roman Empire began to perceive how useless it was to keep on persecuting them.[1] In the end their determination to worship Christ no matter the cost got those Roman Christians the liberty to do so without fear.

Therefore, what should matter most to George and Marie as they negotiate their disagreement is not female submission but justice—what is the fair and right thing to do? This holds whether both are Christians, whether only one partner is, or whether neither is. People sometimes ask me whether it isn't easier for two Christians to negotiate than if one professes no faith. The answer is that negotiation is *never* easy. But sometimes it's more amicable and pleasant than at other times. Does being a Christian contribute to that? It all depends. If George believes in hierarchy, as many Christian men do, and Marie believes in equality, it may not be amicable at all. And, in any case, negotiation is going to be extraordinarily difficult for them both. Since negotiation is the *how* of mutual submission, if a Christian husband does not fully accept the idea that he ought to submit to his wife, he'll never be a creative compromiser.

On the other hand, recall Cheryl and Fred from chapter 3. Both were devout Christians and both egalitarian, that is, they believed in male-female equality. They went through many of the same kinds of struggles that Alice and Harold did, and also arrived at a novel and creative marriage arrangement. In short, having Christian faith or not is *not by itself* the key issue to amicable and pleasant negotiations. The more basic question is, does each person have that passion for justice referred to in chapter 3? Can they go beyond that "first mile" to the "second mile" of love referred to in chapter 2? Unfortunately, we need only to look at Church history and the people around us to know that simply being a Christian doesn't automatically increase the supply of either justice or love, even though we wish it would.

Indeed, being a Christian sometimes stands in the way of justice. That is especially true if one believes that hierarchy is ordained of God. The hierarchy can be *racial*—it is white Christians who maintain the inequalities in South Africa, and it was white American Christians who maintained injustice during slavery and legal segregation. The hierarchy can be also based on *social class*. Many Christians, for instance, opposed the union movement and its concern for justice during the nineteenth and early twentieth centuries. And the hierarchy can be based on *gender*. These are precisely the three areas to which Paul refers in Galatians 3: 28. In Christ, these hierarchies are supposed to be flattened out into bridges of justice and love. Hierarchy people have a hard time building those bridges.

As we think about George and Marie's disagreement, we focus on this basic issue: how do they go about negotiating a fair settlement—one they can both live with comfortably? Their particular disagreement is an example of bargaining in motion. It is taking them a long time trying to resolve it. Meanwhile they are having to live alongside each other and that disagreement. So far they have not been able to make it go away, nor have they been able to work out a solution both can live with, so instead they live with the disagreement.

That's what I mean by negotiation in progress or motion. Many married couples are not accustomed to the idea of *living with* disagreements. The idea of patient negotiation is simply foreign to them. But it's not their fault. A lot of "how to help your marriage" manuals give them the false idea that something's wrong if they can't solve all their marital conflicts. And not just solve them, but immediately, if not sooner. That erroneous idea creates more problems than it solves, and it fits the hierarchy position like a glove. If a couple can't tolerate disagreements or if they think it's sinful to have them, then load the guilt and burden on the woman for protracting them. Let her get rid of her guilt by giving in to her husband.

SOLUTION-DIRECTED BARGAINING

But Marie just finished reading *All We're Meant to Be,* so she's not about to cave in. However, there are two ways to carry on protracted or ongoing negotiations. One way is to do it in an amicable fashion. Another label for the same thing is solution-directed bargaining. We saw this style of bargaining carried on between Alice and Harold. The chief way to identify this style of bargaining is that the partners feel they are making some progress toward solution. There may only be "a light at the end of the tunnel," but at least it's there, and the end seems closer than it was some time ago.

Marie and George are negotiating this way over their disagreement. Both of them feel they are making sure but slow progress toward a mutually satisfactory outcome. Why? What is it about solution-directed bargaining that gives the participants this impression? We learned several characteristics of this bargaining style in chapters 3 and 4. One is following certain rules of "fair play." Another is the conviction that your partner is genuinely interested in maximum *joint* profit, or MJP. A third is flexibility, or the capability to switch bargaining strategies. If a particular strategy is not moving the disagreement off dead center, another is tried.

Distractions

Besides using those features, George and Marie are using several additional techniques characteristic of this bargaining style. One of these might be called "keeping your eye on the ball and ignoring the other person's diversionary moves." In athletics, concentration is a key element. The swimmer, diver, tennis, baseball or basketball player must concentrate totally on what s/he is supposed to do. Opposing athletes and fans often try to distract them by catcalls, the "raspberry," or anything else that is known to rattle a player. But a good athlete knows that "the goal's the thing—forget the distractions."

In marriage, the distraction is not usually intentional, but it is one nonetheless. In the process of trying to come up with some creative compromise to settle their difference, for instance, George suggests to Marie that perhaps they could arrange for alternate weeks: one week the children could stay with him, on the other they could go with her. But Marie was very tired and irritable when George made that offer late one night. And so she reacted with a strategy that is *not* characteristic of solution-directed bargaining, but one that is more characteristic of deadlock-directed bargaining, as I discuss it below.

Marie used a strategy of disparagement—she tried to put George down. She called him and his ideas for compromise "dumb" and "stupid." The kindest things she said were that they were "irrational" and "nonsensical." Now, George could have reacted and spoken to her exactly as she spoke to him—

many spouses do. He could have called her dumb and stupid, and her ideas idiotic. But George simply ignored her comments and kept his eye on the ball, the goal of resolving their conflict. He *concentrated,* rather than react in kind to her disparagement. What he concentrated on was presenting additional reasons why she should accept his compromise.

The next day, Marie apologized for her behavior, and began to continue their discussion. They could have gotten sidetracked from their goal if George had not ignored the distraction, and kept them on track. Ignoring putdowns and concentrating on resolving the problem is a most important feature of solution-directed bargaining. If couples spend most of their time reacting in kind to each other's disparagements, mutually satisfactory solutions will be a long time in coming!

Reconciling

Another way to carry on solution-directed bargaining is through reconciling measures—being a *reconciler.* We saw in chapter 2 that Barnabas tried to be a reconciler—to build bridges between John Mark and Paul—but Paul would have none of it.

Fortunately, Marie is a reconciler. To reconcile is to try to smooth over hurts, pains, sufferings, disappointments, cutting remarks, and so on, that one or both may have inflicted on the other. At this particular juncture, Marie senses it is time to do some reconciling. Even though George overlooked her disparaging comments, she realizes that nonetheless she may have hurt or offended him in some deep ways. She may have undercut his self-image, his self-confidence.

Her apology was the barest beginning. What she also did was to try to probe George to find out whether or not she "cut him to the quick" with her comments. It turns out she didn't. George tells her he didn't take her seriously—he knew she was tired.

In any case, George was too wise a bargainer to pay attention to her comments that his compromises were dumb. George knew they were *good* ideas.

Had Marie really devastated either George or his suggestions or both, her task as reconciler would have been to show George she does respect him and his ideas, that she does take them seriously. As the gospel folk song goes, she wants to "guard his dignity and save his pride." She does want to discuss the compromises, whether or not she agrees with them. That is the kind of bridge that has to be built if serious negotiation is to continue. To be reconciled is like crossing a precipice via a bridge; to be unreconciled is to be separated by a wide chasm. Had George been devastated and had he believed that Marie did not respect either him and/or his ideas, further negotiations could not have taken place. They would have been on their way to a deadlock. But as soon as he became convinced that she believed his suggestions to be worthwhile enough to discuss deeply and seriously, they were closer to a solution than they had been before.

Supportiveness

Very often, part of reconciling is to be extra warm and supportive. It goes without saying that tender, gracious, nurturant words and actions are always an asset during negotiations. Genuine smiles along with a gentle and loving demeanor are always important. But Marie knows they're especially vital while trying to build bridges—to reconcile—so she is particularly warm at this point. And genuinely so. Her motives are not ulterior. She is not a crass manipulator. But in her quest for a just solution, she knows she must show particular nurturance during this stage. Her genuineness is also born out of her sincere concern for George as a human being made in the image of God. She does want God's best for him.

This is a good place to repeat that there is no contradiction between negotiation and nurturance. I say "repeat" because in chapter 2 I tried to show that love and negotiation for justice were quite inseparable. Nurturance is an expression of love and is in no way incompatible with bargaining if we think of it as belonging to the "how" of mutual submission. Marie is being nurturant at the same time that she is being firm in her objectives about Sunday school, her parents, and so on. The image that many people have of a gentle person necessarily being a nonperson is nonsense, and nonbiblical. In the past this image was foisted on women, and unfortunately, some Christians still perpetrate it. Let's hope it soon gains the decent burial it deserves!

The Principle of the Thing

Worrying about "the principle of the thing" is another way *not* to do solution-directed bargaining. Couples who concentrate on the *thing*—the issue they are trying to resolve—are more likely to move closer toward resolution than couples who focus on what they claim is the "principle" behind it! That apparently was Paul's problem in negotiating with Barnabas over Mark. He was so concerned with what he thought was a vital principle that he became unable to work something out with Barnabas for Mark's good. Paul probably defined the principle as teaching Mark a lesson about being a quitter.

I am not saying couples should not have principles in mind when they negotiate, but rather that principles (like things) can get in the way of *people*. You remember that Jesus summed up all the specific rules contained in the Jewish law by two great overriding principles: love your God with all your being and love your neighbor as yourself. Jesus repeatedly set aside specific religious rules for the benefit of people—healing on the sabbath, for one. Again, the great principles that guide our negotiations should be based on love and justice. Those principles are bound to benefit the persons with whom we deal. But that's quite a different matter from the "principle of the thing," which is usually just a specific rule that we think is terribly important.

For example, George may say to Marie, "What I really care about is the *principle* of the thing—families should be together on Sunday." Marie might respond by showing George the specific ways she thinks she and the children would be better off if they could do as she wishes. But no matter what reasons Marie gives him, it doesn't make one iota of difference; he is not willing to compromise his principle. All he will say is that families are "better off together," but he won't say specifically why, or respond to her specific points as to why they would be better off in Sunday school.

Or to turn it around, Marie might say to George, "The principle of the thing is that the kids should be in Sunday school." He might then try to negotiate with her by pointing out specific ways the children would be better off with him. But she refuses to discuss the specific merits of his reasons. It's just the *principle* that she wants to enforce.

Sometimes both marriage partners focus on the "principle of the thing" rather than on the thing itself. That's virtually a sure way *not* to have solution-directed bargaining. The "thing"— the disagreement—will almost never be settled. If only one partner is concerned with the "principle," then it's a little simpler for the other to point out how worrying about a principle keeps them from resolving their disagreement. But if they're *both* worried about principles, pointing out the toothpick in the other person's eye becomes harder to do because of the log in one's own (Matt. 7: 3–5).

In this case, Marie actually did tell George her principle about kids being in Sunday school. George responded, not with another principle but with specifics, giving her concrete reasons why the doctrines and practices of the church she had in mind were not really best for the children. In short, George put people—the children—ahead of a principle, namely, that children should be in Sunday school. He showed Marie how the children could be harmed and hindered in *that* Sunday school, and that they'd actually be better off *not* going there.

At that point Marie saw that she had no way to counter what he had said. George had begun to convince her that her principle was not as persuasive as his reasons. Most of all, she saw that the children's best interests were indeed more important than her principle or rule, so she stopped trying to negotiate that way. The upshot was that Marie, as well as George, was able to avoid being sidetracked by "principles." Instead they could concentrate on trying to arrive at a resolution that would be best for the children in particular, and for her and George as well.

It's for the Children

Incidentally, George's reasoning in this matter introduces us to another bargaining strategy, but one that is not without peril. Recall that in chapter 3, some ways to bargain were called "moral obligation," "promise," or "individual well-being." What George is doing here is saying that Marie should go along with him because *it's best for the children*. This is a strategy couples often use when they're trying to decide matters of child discipline, child-training, what school district they should live in, what friends and social life the child should have, and so forth.

It's a very common strategy and, like any other strategy, whether it leads to resolution or not depends on when and how it's used. But watch out: it's such a convenient cloak to hide one's true reasons for wanting one's spouse to stop or start doing something. If your spouse says, "Let's do this because it's best for the children," that can make you or anyone else feel guilty and uncertain. After all, who's against children?

But if you invoke the children's well-being simply to mask your true motives, that in the long run does not contribute to amicable bargaining. To try to hide one's genuine reasons is not negotiating according to the rules of fair play referred to in chapter 3. Fair play demands honesty in voicing one's actual reasons, complaints, objections, or whatever has to do with the particular disagreement. The reason for that kind of honesty is that if your spouse doesn't realize your true reasons, s/he may, in good faith, negotiate on the basis of what you've said when that really isn't the issue at all. Therefore, all that energy and attempt at creative compromise are being wasted because of not getting to the real objections.

Moreover, when and if your spouse discovers your ulterior motive s/he will not only have a right to be angry because you haven't "played fair," s/he might even start questioning your concern for maximum *joint* profit. Your spouse might begin to feel that you were more concerned for maximum *individual* profit. S/he might reason that your lack of forthrightness represents an attempt to try to "put something over" on him/her. That might not be the case at all, but covering up motives and not bargaining according to the rules of fair play are bound to create that impression.

For example, Mike says to Beth, who wants to take a full-time job, "When our children come home from school, you should be there to greet them and hear what they have to say." He tells her she shouldn't work, and he uses the children's best interests as the reason. But after Beth negotiates with Mike on that basis for a while she discovers that his real reason for not wanting her to work is that she will earn as much in her job as he earns in his. He believes her equal earnings will threaten his position as "head of the home," and he was using the children to mask his actual concern. But it took a lot of wasted time and energy before Beth found that out.

In contrast to Mike, George was forthright with his wife, Marie, about focusing on their children's interests. And Marie realized that fact, just as surely as it finally dawned on Beth that Mike, in contrast, was covering up his true reasons. Being candid and straightforward throughout every phase of ongoing negotiations is a sure way to keep on the track of solution-directed bargaining. To be anything less is to risk drifting away from amicable negotiation and toward deadlock-directed bargaining.

George was also open and honest enough to tell Marie that the children's interests were not the *sole* reason he didn't want them to go to that particular church. In addition, he likes to have the children with him because he enjoys them, and that was one reason he offered the compromise mentioned earlier for the children to alternate weeks with each parent. In other words, when a parent negotiates in terms of the best interests of the child, s/he may simultaneously hold another reason (for example, his or her own interests) that is equally compelling. There is nothing wrong with that. That is fair play if both reasons are openly stated. And it's fair play as long as concerns for the children are genuine and can be justified under probing, as was the case when Marie probed George.

Trust

An important current running through much of this and the previous chapters has been somewhat overlooked because so many other points had to be made. But now as we discuss solution-directed bargaining, it's time to bring this idea into full view. I'm talking about something called *trust*. The idea of trust is central to the Christian faith. We trust Christ for salvation; we trust his sovereign providence to care for us throughout time and eternity. A common way to define trust is the conscious willingness to risk dependence on another. To trust someone is to rely on that person to the extent of risking loss if s/he doesn't follow through.

For example, you may have a friend who says, "Let's start a car pool to save money and energy. I'll pick you up for work at 7:30." You know from past dealings with your friend that s/he will be there so you don't object when your spouse takes your car at 7:00 A.M. You're now at risk of being late for work if your friend doesn't show, but you know that won't happen. In short, you trust her/him.

Trust is an element that is essential to resolving conflicts. Alice and Harold trusted each other. Each knew that s/he could count on the other to carry out his/her part of the bargain they had struck. Harold could rely on Alice, and Alice on Harold, to do everything they said they would do in regard to Alice's going off to seminary.

Trust is also essential while still struggling to work out solutions. In the presence of trust, each person is freer to come up with more creative and innovative resolutions. They won't be thinking, "Well, that's a possible way to settle our disagreement, but I really can't be sure my spouse would follow through on what s/he promises, so why bother suggesting it?" Mistrust contributes to deadlocks because creativity is stifled; trust helps steer couples toward solutions.

Remember that George had proposed a compromise involving a great deal of trust. Whether Marie insists on taking the children to the Sunday school she originally had in mind or to another one, he is willing to alternate Sundays. He trusts Marie not to renege on something she has agreed to do. She won't say, "Even though I took the kids last Sunday, the church is having something special and I want to take them two weeks in a row." By the same token, Marie also trusts George. If he agrees to the bargain, he won't say, "Even though the kids were with me last Sunday, it would be nice if we could go camping again this week."

In chapter 2 love and justice were seen to be two sides of the same coin. Likewise, maximum joint profit and trust are two parts of the same picture. One part is, "Does s/he really want what's best for both of us? Is s/he genuinely concerned for my best interests; or is s/he selfishly looking out solely for what s/he wants? How serious is s/he about the 'nuts and bolts' of mutual submission?"

The second part is, "How much can I count on him/her to *keep on* looking out for my interests by keeping up the agreements we work out?" There is some research evidence, for instance, showing that while husbands will often promise their wives they will do certain household chores—repairs, cleaning, washing, painting, etc.—they never seem to be able to "get around" to them.[2] These husbands are hardly proving trustworthy, at least as far as chores are concerned.

Whether or not you see your spouse wanting maximum joint profit represents the situation up till now—it is your assessment of the past and present. But trust is your assessment of the *future*. And it doesn't take too long to figure out that the future is a direct extension of the past. Wives and husbands who show their spouses that they are working for the good of *both* of them inspire their spouses to trust and have confidence in them. In contrast, husbands and wives who make their spouses feel they are aiming at selfish profit stir up mistrust and suspicion. The fact is that on the one hand, maximum joint profit, trust, and resolution-directed bargaining cluster together. But on the other hand, it is equally true that seeking for selfish profit, mistrust, and deadlock-directed bargaining cluster together just as strongly.

THE IMPORTANCE OF PATIENCE

In this chapter I have discussed additional strategies—more ways that couples can deal with conflict. "But if that is the case" someone asks, "doesn't the chapter title sound rather strange? Shouldn't knowing how to negotiate help us solve all our disagreements?" While we all wish it could work that way, unfortunately it doesn't, because of some of the inherent human frailties already discussed in chapters 1 and 2. We tend to be selfish, greedy, and untrusting of others even when we don't want to be. Often we're not even aware that what we're doing is causing our partner to feel hurt or unjustly treated. "Why do I step on your toe when I don't even know I'm doing it?"

Yet somehow Christians have created a myth that marriages and churches and mission groups, and so on, should have no unsettled disagreements. Indeed, it is considered "unspiritual" even to allow discontent to stir within one's breast, much less let it surface. If it does surface, it should be "worked out" immediately.

Friends, often called Quakers, have a lot to teach the rest of us about patience in working out disagreements. Friends never vote to settle disagreements during their business meetings. Neither do they adhere to any hierarchical approach whatsoever in resolving differing points of view. Instead, they keep on talking until all present agree that there is a "unity of mind and heart" as to what to do (or not to do). This "unity" is also called a "weight" or "sense" of the meeting. Some discussions take a long, long time before that "sense" is actually achieved. But that doesn't seem to bother Friends. They are convinced that God's will is discerned more perfectly through living and grappling with disagreements than by quick appeals to a chain of command.

Persons who adhere to some form of marital hierarchy perpetrate an unreal and, I think, unbiblical view of human relations that sees healthy or strong marriage relationships as being free of struggle, pain, and suffering. *That image itself is faulty*— life is simply not like that. They seem to be ignoring the fact that all human relations are marked by pain and struggle, but, it is to be hoped, by development and maturity. Family relations involve effort similar to that of the athlete training for the Olympics, the musician preparing for a performance. Effective social relations involve struggling against inertia—against muscles that won't respond, against distractions that constantly enter in to keep us from the single-minded goal to do things better, to make those relationships better. Wanting "better" is not necessarily selfish. The worker labors for his/her family to provide for them in more than just a material sense. We surely want children to have food and clothes, but we also want to enrich them through such things as buying them a good book or taking them to a fine play or concert.

Struggling to make family relations "better" gives us great satisfaction because it draws on our creative energies. We are made in the image of God; and what is more characteristic of God than to create? It also gives us satisfaction because we know we are serving others; and what is more characteristic of God in Christ than to serve?

In their effort to shut out the pains of human struggle, the advocates of hierarchy risk losing out on the joys of development by shoring up their faulty image of marriage with a rickety structure. "Make the husband the head (leader, initiator, etc.)," they say, "and all will be well." But how can there be any struggle and pain and thus growth if the woman is passive? Single women who would like to interest a male in a "relationship" are frequently advised to do "nothing" if he doesn't seem enthused.[3] But the male is usually told to take "action" if he's interested in a particular female. Such writers are training singles in the hierarchical approach to female-male relations. When female readers marry, they may find themselves following advice like this: "Turn the whole business over to God. . . . He doesn't need any advice or help from you." *If you're a woman, that is.* But apparently God needs help and advice from the male: "If you're the man . . . of course, God may expect some action from you."[4]

But if some writers convey a faulty vision of marriage (struggle-free through female submission), what is a better vision? Chapter 1 has shown how the hierarchical vision can stifle the woman and stagnate the marriage. An equal-partner marriage, however, permits each partner full and free expression of what they are and hope to be; it also permits the marriage arrangements themselves to be adventuresome, creative, exciting, innovative, dynamic, and open to change. Chapter 7 calls it the vision of the "examined marriage." Everything we've covered in prior chapters contributes to that vision. The present chapter is no exception even though the idea of coexisting with conflict may seem to contradict that idea.

However, there really is no contradiction. Every cook knows that a special meal takes a long time to prepare. Cooking is a process—a series of steps during which we must be careful and patient while working toward a final product. The same is true if we're building a chest of drawers or a cabinet. In either cooking or building, we might sometimes make mistakes that are frustrating and costly. Yet, we must keep on working and aiming toward a satisfactory outcome. Marital negotiations are often just like that.

6.
MARITAL DEADLOCKS

FOR QUITE SOME time Dana and Andy have been discussing a problem they face as parents of a pre-teen daughter. Though they've both been patient up to now, it looks like they're heading toward a deadlock. Andy is growing weary of the discussions about how Jill should behave and what she should wear now that she's approaching puberty. Since he believes in male leadership, he finally says, "Dana, this is it. Here's how we have to handle the situation, so let's stop discussing it. There's no use pushing it any further." Andy is imposing a solution; he's coercing Dana. And what's more, he doesn't want to "waste" any more time and energy talking to her about it. Dana does not agree. She feels their problem is far from being solved in a fair and equitable manner. It is obvious to her that Andy is trying to use his authority as a male to terminate the discussions, and she resents it terribly. The advocates of hierarchy would side with Andy, of course, and would deny that he is engaging in the unpleasant and unbiblical idea of domination by arguing that Dana should "submit in love." They believe Dana should look on Andy's behavior as "God's way of teaching and dealing with her."

But Dana does not accept that particular view of male-female relationships. Instead she is persuaded that a central theme of the Bible is one we discussed earlier, namely, that justice and love are two sides of the same coin.

Dana accordingly tells Andy that she feels anger because he's trying to dominate—to exercise raw male power, and that he is not practicing *mutual submission,* which she sees as central to Christian marriage. The Moravians had a way of deciding tough problems called "the drawing of the Lot." Based on Acts 1: 23–26, the procedure was for the Elders to put three wood and paper reeds—one labeled "Ja" or "yes," another labeled "Nein" or "no," and a third blank) into a wooden bowl. Drawing the blank meant that they should not take any action. "The Lot was nothing more than an extension of prayer—to be resorted to only after they had exhausted their own repertoire of possible solutions to a tough problem."[1] The Moravians no longer follow that technique, and I certainly don't recommend it. But the practice does illustrate a sensitivity on the part of Apostles and Moravians to the reality that appeals to hierarchy to solve problems are at their core unsatisfactory and unsatisfying. Such appeals create more problems than they solve; there are better ways. But because Andy holds to a chain of command, while Dana sees it as futility, they have landed right in the middle of a deadlock.

Agreeing to Disagree

Whether we like to admit it or not, virtually every marriage has or has experienced one or more deadlocks. Remember that Harold and Alice had a long-standing deadlock over her being a part of their church's women's program. They had agreed years ago to disagree and leave it at that (but not be disagreeable about it). Their *mutual decision* to stop talking about it was quite explicit. Alice told Harold that's how she wanted it, and he concurred. However, many couples aren't quite that direct or "up front" about disagreements.

For instance, about a year prior to Andy's current attempt to dominate Dana in this ongoing disagreement they both sensed that the other didn't want to talk about it for a while. Each could pick up cues and clues from what the other said that a "cooling off" period was in order. Unlike Alice, who had been direct with Harold, Dana and Andy had been indirect with each other.

The effect in either case is the same—deadlock. Each partner strongly disagrees with the other's proposed solution. But, for a while at least, neither wants to push the matter. They're postponing any further negotiation "indefinitely," or else till "next week," "next month," or "this summer."

Throughout this book I have stressed the idea that in themselves marital disagreements and conflicts are not unhealthy. Contrary to the usual idea that conflicts are "bad," they may often be a sign of marital vigor. Conflicts help bring changes into a marriage that make it responsive to the shifting needs, desires, goals, and aspirations of the partners. Instead of growing stale, the relationship stays as fresh and dynamic as the constantly growing persons.

But if the conflicts aren't resolved and those healthy changes don't come about, what then? How healthy is that?

No one would disagree that the most desirable situation is to have no unresolved conflicts in a marriage. The whole idea of this and the prior chapters is to provide ideas, insights, and strategies in order to avoid deadlocks. Negotiation is the process of learning how "to submit mutually to one another," how to compromise so as to reach solutions that are positive for both partners—that make each one "feel good" about the solution.

But no one is all-wise or perfect and sometimes couples can't seem to reach a compromise. We may not like this reality, but it's one that we need to acknowledge and face squarely. Putting the matter on the back burner and agreeing to disagree may be a healthy way to cope, at least for a while.

Time, of course, is a key factor. Remember in chapter 3 that Alice *could not* wait indefinitely. But in Dana's case, the conflict was one that did not demand an immediate solution. So long as her daughter was only eleven or twelve she felt she could wait a while to try to reach a compromise with Andy.

Andy believes that when a girl reaches puberty she should stop acting like a tomboy. Instead of jeans and tee shirts, she should wear dresses and start acting like a "Christian lady." As Jill becomes more of an adolescent and very aware of peer pressure, she resents having to wear dresses to school when all the other girls wear jeans and shirts or sweaters. For Jill's sake, Dana can no longer let the matter lie fallow; she feels the conflict must be resolved as soon as possible.

Besides time, a second key factor in deciding how long to let an unresolved problem lie dormant is its basic importance. Alice's was all-important to her, and Dana feels her conflict with Andy is all-important to Jill's normal development as a mature human being. Dana feels that forcing an adolescent to wear clothes so out of keeping with her surroundings could forever damage her self-esteem and self-confidence. Further, it could sour Jill on the Christian message which her father insists is the basis for his command.

Unilateral Action

One great danger in trying to dominate as Andy is trying to do is that, when you think you've got the situation just exactly the way you want it (often against the wishes of others), you can lose control completely. Dana can't get Andy to compromise their deadlock. Time is precious and the matter is vital, so she simply buys Jill the clothes she wants to wear and sends her off to school in them. Andy has to leave for work before

Jill gets dressed for school so he doesn't find out about the *accomplished fact* till that evening. What should or could Andy do? Spank Jill? Get violent with Dana? Order them both to cease and desist?

Dana broke the deadlock by going ahead and doing what she thought was best, in spite of Andy's attempt to dominate. And in many marriages, that sort of unilateral or one-sided action happens far more often than any of us would like to admit. We all know marriages in which the wife dutifully says, "My husband is the head of the house, *but* sometimes I have to go ahead anyhow and do something of which he does not approve." Unilateral action on the part of either spouse is not an ideal way to break a deadlock because it causes a lot of hostility and resentment. Andy feels what Dana and Jill have done is unfair, and he resents it. . . . But Dana felt exactly the same way about Andy's behavior in prohibiting the jeans.

A second reason unilateral action is not ideal is that it's almost always a win-lose situation, like a ballgame. When conflicts are resolved through mutual submission or compromise, each party gets something—neither loses. Here Andy has lost, so he may try to figure out some way to undercut Dana and Jill—to make them lose so that he can win what to him has become a deadly serious contest. Through some unilateral action (for instance, canceling the charge accounts used to pay for Jill's clothes) he may indeed sabotage them; but then they may turn around and surprise him a second time. Those devious moves and countermoves could go on indefinitely like the plots of B-movies or mediocre TV shows. Unfortunately, a series of such moves seldom contributes to trusting, loving relationships.

Shock Value

Sometimes, however, unilateral moves can shock a spouse into realizing how deeply the other person feels about some matter. Had Andy been sensitive to Dana (and Jill), he would have realized that for Dana to do something that drastic—to take that much of a risk of upsetting their overall marriage relationship—she must have felt very strongly about Jill's situation. Instead of feeling sorry for himself that he "lost," or trying to figure out ways to reestablish his "male headship," he would do much better immediately to negotiate some kind of mutually acceptable compromise—something that all three of them could live with.

Unilateral moves may occasionally shock the unyielding partner into solution-directed bargaining. For that reason, while not recommended, it may sometimes be the only way a terribly frustrated partner can hope to shake his/her spouse into negotiating for equity and justice.

The foregoing discussion makes it plain that agreeing to disagree over deadlocks—postponing pushing them—can sometimes be a healthy way to deal with them, especially if time is not at a premium, or if the matter has a lower priority or importance than some other matters. The question then naturally arises as to how many deadlocks a marriage can sustain before it threatens to become unglued. No one knows for sure. Some marriages, for example, might be able to sustain a dozen deadlocks over matters that each partner considers relatively less important than some other things. Other marriages might not be able to survive even one, if either or both partners feel very deeply about it. How long could Harold and Alice's marriage have survived if they had deadlocked indefinitely over her going on to seminary?

DEADLOCK-DIRECTED BARGAINING

Bargaining towards a deadlock is something nobody wants to do, yet we tend to do it far too often. It's exactly the opposite of everything constructive that we have been examining. It's not seeing "light at the end of the tunnel"; it's not amicable; and it can be downright unpleasant. While the bargaining is not yet at a stalemate, one has the feeling of edging closer to it all the time.

Chapter 5 showed that seeking selfish profit and generating mistrust contribute to deadlock-directed negotiation, as does failure to concentrate on rules of fair play or on ways to be flexible. Deadlocks can also become imminent through failure to concentrate on the problem to be solved and, instead, allowing yourself to get distracted—your spouse puts you down so, in return, you put him/her down. Or instead of concentrating on your spouse's well-being, you concentrate (as Andy did) on *principles* that get in the way of *people*. Or deadlocks may loom because one or both spouses fail to concentrate on reconciliation—on rectifying past mistakes and building bridges of respect. And deadlocks may appear imminent if one or both spouses are not as completely honest and forthright as they can possibly be about *what* they want and *why* they want it.

Notice how often the word *concentrate* appears above; and it is certainly implicit in everything that is being said. Creative conflict and negotiation is not easy—it's hard work. What is easy is simply to take the path of least resistance and let the household revolve around one person. The other spouse (usually the female) simply ceases to negotiate for justice; s/he just gives in to "keep the peace." But couples who want something richer and more satisfying than that will find ample reward for the struggle and the concentration negotiation takes.

Toughness

Besides those routes already discussed, couples find themselves moving towards deadlock via some additional routes as well. One of these is called *toughness*. Though the term may sound offensive, it refers to something we all understand and experience. How much am I prepared to ask my spouse to sacrifice for me? How much do I want from him/her? How much am I prepared to scale down (compromise) what I want? In turn, what sacrifices does my spouse want from me? How much does s/he want? How much is s/he prepared to scale down or compromise?

Those of us who lived in the Midwest and East during the 1977–78 coal strike know firsthand what can happen when each side asks a great deal of the other, and then is reluctant to scale down what they ask. In the past, marriage gave the husband the right to ask much of the woman. He expected her to give up a great deal on his behalf. To be sure, few women or men thought of what was going on as a sacrifice on her part, or that he was being tough. But suppose a woman had said, "I don't want to change my name when we marry. I'll keep mine; or else we'll hyphenate our names; or perhaps you might want to take my name. And the children can take our hyphenated name, or perhaps my name."

Had a woman said those things twenty, thirty, or more years ago, we can be almost certain that virtually all husbands would have resisted strongly—they *would* have been tough. They would rarely, if ever, have compromised on that matter. They wanted women to make the sacrifice of giving up their own name even if women didn't want to. But why? There's no Bible verse commanding it. However, it is a powerful social custom of which most people approve. The man feels justified in saying, "It's a matter of principle; it's the 'right and proper' thing to do."

But today some women respond that that principle stands in the way of their own personhood. Marsha, for instance, says to her fiancé, Joel, that it's too great a sacrifice to ask her to give up her name. It represents her identity as an autonomous person, just as Joel's name does for him. Joel could be tough and refuse to budge from his conviction that she should take his name. If she is equally intransigent, they are doing deadlock-directed bargaining, moving toward an impasse. But Joel tempers the sacrifice he expects from Marsha, and settles for a hyphenated name. He submits to her in this matter.

Something else men have always asked of women is for wives to move with them when they take a new job—whether as minister or truckdriver, businessman or factory worker. Women and children tore up their roots and left their friends because they felt it was best for the men, although, since the husbands supported them, they really didn't have much choice. But what will Alice and Harold do if some day they're both serving different churches in the same community and Harold receives a call to leave while Alice feels God wants her to remain where she is? How tough and unyielding will each be? How much sacrifice will each ask of the other?

Quite apart from these major issues are numerous daily ways in which wives and husbands are tough with—ask sacrifices of—each other. A husband wants to watch his favorite team; the wife wants him to watch the children instead. He wants her to stop spending so much money. She wants him to stop spending so much time with his friends, or his job, or his church work, and spend more time with her. The list of such sacrifices we ask of our spouses can grow quite long and sometimes humorous. A woman I know, for instance, asks her husband to sleep in another room because his snoring keeps her awake!

But whatever the matter is, you must weigh carefully how tough you actually want to be. If the loving thing for your spouse to do requires considerable sacrifice on his or her part, don't be the least bit fearful to press for those sacrifices, just as Alice and also Marsha did. But keep in mind that Alice, always the creative compromiser, was willing to make sacrifices of her own to avoid a deadlock. Save your greatest toughness for the things that matter most to you. On as many matters as practicable be as yielding as possible; that is, be willing to sacrifice or compromise as much as you can.

If you and your spouse are really concerned for maximum joint profit, such sacrificial behavior on the part of either of you is almost certain to generate reciprocal sacrifices. This is the essence of what mutual submission is all about: each making sacrifices for the other, yet neither fearful of calling on the other to make sacrifices. That kind of mutuality is surely part of what Jesus had in mind when he said, "Give and it shall be given to you" (Luke 6: 38). In contrast, a lot of toughness on a lot of matters on your part is likely to stimulate a lot of toughness by your spouse. Mutual toughness carried to the point of intransigence is one of the surest ways to arrive at deadlocks.

Withdrawal

Another type of behavior that often moves couples toward deadlock is well known to anyone who has read or thought much about communication skills. Some people call it "withdrawal" or "clamming up." Sometimes one or both partners will simply stop negotiating while they're still in the process of trying to work something out, or arrive at a settlement. They may or may not physically withdraw from each other, but socially there's no live connection between them. They're not actively involved in any ongoing give-and-take processes.

There is some research evidence to suggest that husbands may withdraw from wives more frequently than wives withdraw from husbands. Some counselors see this difference as part of a larger problem that men have in being expressive in general— in simply talking over things about which they feel or care very deeply. Recent widespread public attention to *men's* liberation and the importance of expressing their true feelings may have helped some men overcome that inhibiting disability. But in any case when either or both partners "clam up," constructive compromise is inevitably delayed.

Forget It

Something else that men seem to do more often than women is to try to get their wives to "forget it." When either spouse begins (as Andy did) by saying to the other: "These discussions are taking too long, they're too painful, they're wearing me out, they're setting up a barrier between us," the same spouse usually continues by saying, "Let's go back to square one, to where we were before we had all these discussions and arguments." In effect, s/he is saying, "Let's go back to the status quo; let's forget all about the changes we were trying to negotiate."

Harold, for example, could have said to Alice, "Forget your plans to go to seminary to become a minister. Just stay where you are; be content and accept your present challenges. It's too much hassle to try to work this problem out. It'll be a lot simpler if you just set those ideas aside." Usually the spouse who wants a return to what the situation was before all the discussion came up, is *not* the one who wanted any changes in the first place. Harold was going along—living his life—and preferred things to go on just as they always had. It is the partner (Alice) who brought up the matter in the first place who wants the changes. It is certain that Alice does not want the status quo. The problem is that if the spouse who wants the status quo persists in wanting it, s/he becomes too concerned with that to think about creative compromise. The upshot is that preoccupation with the status quo edges couples towards deadlocks. That partner is so busy thinking about what was, he or she can't visualize what could be.

There is a further problem that always seems to be part of status quo "nonsolutions." Since nonsolutions don't genuinely resolve anything, the issue in question tends to pop up repeatedly either in the same form or perhaps with some variation.

If, in October, Harold had actually been able to get Alice to forget her plans, she probably would have brought them up all over again by December. Nonsolutions do just that—solve nothing. The root issue has to be dealt with, not merely buried to confront us another day.

Stop It

There is a thin but significant line between, on the one hand, trying to get your partner to "forget it" and, on the other hand, actually saying "Shut up," "Stop bringing it up," "I never want to hear about it again," "The matter is closed—period." We just saw Harold making a *request* of Alice: "Would you *please* forget the changes you have in mind?" But that is quite a different story from one in which a spouse tries to *order* his/her partner (as Andy did) to "stop it." In this situation the idea is to *suppress* his/her desire to negotiate—to *coerce* the spouse against his/her will. Again, men seem to have a record of doing this more frequently than women. And hierarchical views of male leadership, authority, and initiative contribute to this sort of nonsolution, just as they do to the status quo variety.

7.

AVOIDING DEADLOCKS AND STAGNATION: THE EXAMINED MARRIAGE

IN SPITE OF all the prayer and planning that most couples do, in spite of all their hard work during bargaining and their attempts at mutual submission, sometimes divorce becomes an increasingly haunting possibility. At marriage no Christian ever thinks that he or she could divorce the grand person with whom vows are being exchanged. But sometimes after a while the unthinkable becomes a live but painful option to contemplate.

There are *many* reasons people get divorced. Accumulated deadlocks is often *one* of them. *One* way to stay married is to *avoid getting into deadlocks over issues that matter a great deal to you, and/or where time is a crucial factor in the decision.* Similarly, if you're single, one way to avoid a divorce-prone marriage is to try to figure out *beforehand* if you and your prospective partner can negotiate so as to avoid deadlocks. (More is said about singles in chapters 8 and 9.)

But how is that done? What can a couple do to avoid or minimize the likelihood of deadlocks? Is there some peg on which to hang all the negotiating principles presented in the preceding chapters, some shorthand way to help me to fit them all together? Is there some overall vision, or image, or idea of what my spouse and I can do to avoid deadlocks?

There is, and while it's no *guarantee* of avoiding deadlocks, when considered in conjunction with the earlier specifics, it provides a basis for eventually resolving deadlocks when they do surface. The vision or basic idea required is this: we need to think of marriage not as a *state,* and not even as a steady *relationship,* but instead as a *process,* or relationship in process. As you read these words you're probably seated. Is your chair moving? Or if you're standing, is the floor moving? They don't seem to be, but the physicists tell us that matter is made up of tiny molecules that are constantly in motion. So, while the wall over there seems to be standing still, it really isn't.

Snapshot or Motion Picture?

Most of us would like marriage to be as steady and predictable as that wall appears to be. It's much more comfortable to think of the wall and marriage as standing still—as being like a snapshot. Many children's tales end with a snapshot captioned: "They all lived happily ever after." But is marriage really like a snapshot? Or is it more like motion picture film in which the camera catches a series of clips that together make up a coherent scene?

Some people would like to make their marriages a type of snapshot. They would like to capture a certain pose between themselves and their spouse and just "hold it" till "death do them part." They work very hard to maintain their set ideas of exactly what a marriage should be.

A lot of other people simply never give the matter much thought. They merely assume that whatever is in the snapshot, "this is what a husband is supposed to do, and not supposed to do"; "this is what a wife is supposed to and not supposed to do." But they've never really discussed the matters with their spouses. Why should they? "Everybody knows" that a husband is supposed to work, that couples should have children, that mothers should be mainly responsible for their care, and that wives should be mainly responsible for housework, and so on and so forth. Likewise, "everybody knows" what couples should do about sex; how couples should relate to friends, to their relatives, to their church, to their children; how couples should spend money, and so on. At least many Christians think "everybody knows," including their spouses, but they never bother to actually find out. They never bother to *talk* about it.

But whether a person works at maintaining set ideas, or whether s/he simply assumes they are set and require no discussion, the couple could very easily be on the road to eventual deadlocks. Dana and Andy's story, as well as Harold and Alice's, make it plain that deadlocks don't erupt overnight; they take time to develop. And the first stages of their development often involve either insisting on set ideas or else simply assuming that all is well, so why "rock the boat"?

Why is that true? Why is it that either set ideas or else somnolence can give birth to deadlocks? Because life and therefore marriage is not a snapshot—it is a moving picture. "Humans are like a dream, like grass which is renewed in the morning: in the morning it flourishes and is renewed; in the evening it fades and withers" (Ps. 90: 5–6, RSV).

Surprises

That life is indeed a motion picture is the mood created by this Scripture. Persons and their surroundings are in constant movement, continual flux. Accordingly, your wife/husband is also changing. Her/his world—his/her vision of Christ and how to serve Him in the world—all these things are being altered, if ever so slightly or subtly. As a result, the things that matter most to him/her are in process—they're changing. If you have set ideas about what marriage should be, or if you are merely indifferent to change, you may be unaware and insensitive to what's happening with your spouse.

Consequently, you may be taken completely by surprise when s/he "suddenly" announces, "I'd like to go back to school," or, "Let's take separate vacations this year." To you the unexpected suggestion seems rash and perhaps out of character, but it probably wasn't so sudden at all. You just hadn't been looking for it or anything like it. And because you have been taken off guard, you may find it hard to negotiate the kind of equity and justice considered in earlier chapters. Thus the result may turn out to be deadlock.

And not only is your spouse changing, you're changing too. Have you given that much thought? Equally important, have you *talked* about those changes with your spouse? Is it possible you will someday catch your spouse unaware because you were changing your ideas about marriage, vocation, use of your talents, or whatever—and keeping them hushed up? Could deadlock be the result?

The Risks of Sameness

"But, oh," you say, "you're not describing me, nor my wife/husband. We don't change—we're the same now as we were when we got married two, five, ten, twenty, or more years ago. We don't have to worry about that problem." And indeed that's possible. We all know couples who seem to act exactly the same way toward each other, and toward other people, as they did when they first got married. And since they stayed married, does that mean one way to avoid divorce is to resist change?

The answer is no, because couples who stay the same and never change run a great risk of marital stagnation. They may remain together, but it is difficult for anyone to discover any zest or dynamic in their marriage. During the late '60s and early '70s a great many young people were complaining about the stagnation they claimed they saw in their parent's marriages, and indeed in many marriages of people over thirty. So they began experimenting with what they thought were new forms of marriage and family to try to capture and maintain the kind of dynamic and zest they thought should be intrinsic to them.

Family Experiments

Communes were one such family experiment, and a goodly number of Christian youth formed their own communes to try to live a simple lifestyle, and also to have an enriched family life. Is that particular kind of change the answer to deadlocks or stagnation? Not by itself, because the sad fact is that most Christian communities have adopted their own set ways of doing things, and those ways are just as rigid as the set ways practiced by the more traditional American household consisting of husband, wife and children. For example, in most Christian communes that I know anything about, men exercise ultimate authority. Women have no more power in those large group-families than they did when they lived outside a community.

Casting about for some ready-made pattern into which we can neatly fit does not seem to be the solution for either dilemma (deadlock or stagnation). We should indeed learn from other's attempts to be creative in coping with change and with the idea of marriage in process. But *there is no one best or final solution.* Instead somebody else's creativity becomes the foundation on which to construct our own dynamic marital relationship in process.

The United States Constitution

Take, as an example, the American constitution. The people who fashioned it learned a great deal from ancient democratic experiments in Greece and Rome. They also knew the pitfalls of the monarchies that had existed in Europe for over a thousand years. What the framers produced was a document that is extraordinary in many respects. Let's just look at two aspects and note their relevance for marriage.

First is the idea of the balance of power among the Congress, the President, and the Courts. Some Christians are fond of saying that families have to have a final authority (naturally, the male) just as they think the U.S. government does. By this they usually mean the President, but in fact the President's authority can be severely limited by Congress and the Supreme Court. And ultimately, of course, he/she can be put out of office by a greater authority—the voters. On the other hand, the President can veto bills the Congress passes; and the Supreme Court can nullify laws passed by Congress and signed by the President. But the Congress and the states can amend the constitution so that the Court can't rule something unconstitutional.

Since all three branches of government have equal capability to stymie the other two, there is no one ultimate unquestioned and unaccountable authority in the U.S. government any more than there need be in marriage. (As we saw in chapter 1, this conclusion applies anywhere—sports, churches, business.) What then keeps government going? What prevents constant deadlocks?

Negotiation!

The persons in government continually try to resolve their differences in ways that will, ideally, bring the most benefit to the most people. And if someone tries to be selfish, someone else is there to call that to their attention, and to everybody else's as well. Little more needs to be said about that idea of stability and order based on justice, because that perspective has been applied to marriage throughout prior chapters.

A Living Document

But there is a second feature of the United States constitution that relates to the vision of marriage that Christians need to cultivate—a vision of marriage in process. And that feature is that the constitution was purposely designed to be a living document in process. The framers fashioned it so that it could be changed in any and all ways. In fact, the whole constitution, including the Bill of Rights, can be completely replaced by something else. This can be done most readily by a provision in the constitution allowing for a convention to meet and draft a whole new constitution.

Why did the framers take such a risk so as to allow the possibility that their marvelous handiwork might one day be discarded? There are many reasons, but the basic one is this: they hoped that the passion for justice, freedom, and order upon which they built the first American constitution would prevail among Americans of later generations. Therefore they believed that any changes made in the constitution, or any new constitution that might one day emerge, would enhance and not detract from justice, freedom, and order.

Total Flexibility

That is the kind of vision of marriage we need to have in order to minimize the chances both of deadlocks and stagnation. For Christians, this idea of total flexibility—this willingness for ultimate mutual submission—is limited only by the belief that marriage ought to be made up of one man and one woman who have pledged before God their sexual exclusivity to one another. There are no additional set ideas about any aspect of marriage that Christians need to carry around in their heads. Flexibility, experimentation, variation, creativity: these are the watchwords of the examined marriage—the marriage in process, the marriage in which mutual submission is fully carried out, marriages such as Harold and Alice's, or Fred and Cheryl's.

It seems quite plain that if total flexibility (within the above limits) is the basic norm, there is nothing a couple could not potentially do in their marriage to achieve or maintain zest and delight in each other. Everything and anything is negotiable. And furthermore, once negotiated, it is not fixed or set. It can be discussed and negotiated again, and later on, yet again.

That kind of vision of marriage does not imply chaos, disorder, or immaturity, any more than does the vision behind the constitution. One reason we have never had to be divorced from the old constitution in favor of a new one is that it is continually being amended in response to new circumstances and new demands. A second reason is that the Congress and courts make new laws and new rulings that continually reflect changing times. And when they make a wrong decision, they are eventually forced to change it. In 1858 the Supreme Court said black slaves were mere property and as such had no civil rights. The Court has come a long way since then! The United States has had such a stable government because for two centuries it has been such a *changing*, nonstagnant government.

Marriages that want to be both stable and stimulating (nonstagnant) must be continually changing. The orderly change comes about through the techniques discussed earlier. The bedrock foundation of this process is total and unrestricted flexibility—flexibility to negotiate any kinds of arrangements so long as they reflect justice, freedom, and order; flexibility growing out of that passion for justice discussed in chapter 3. When we are that flexible—that willing for unrestricted mutual submission to our wife/husband—then we are walking the "second mile of love" referred to in chapter 2.

The Breath of the Spirit

Christians often like to talk about the Holy Spirit moving about in ways completely unexpected and unplanned. We like to pray that He will break in and disrupt dull, humdrum existence wherever it exists and replace it with new life. But it's not certain that we really mean it when we pray that way, say, about the organized church. In any case, we seldom pray that way about marriage. But why not start doing precisely that? As we shall see in the next chapter, God is not bound by any of society's conventions, rules, social roles, customs, niceties, or expectations. Why not ask him to show you and your spouse what new and different and exciting ways he has for your marriage?

There's plenty of precedent for it. In spite of all the social rules and roles that men have created to keep women at a disadvantage, God's Spirit has sometimes been able to break through and give us a radiant glimpse of the new order behind Paul's declaration: "In Christ there is neither male nor female" (Gal. 3: 28). For instance, the Spirit of God erupted and, of all things, made a *woman* both a prophet and a ruler of ancient Israel (Judg. 4: 4–5). Moreover, Deborah replaced a quivering male general and led Israel's army into battle and victory.

In the 1560s another woman believed the Spirit of God was moving her to emulate Deborah. Upon the murder of her brother-in-law general, Jeanne d'Albert led an army of French Huguenots into battle in a religious war. Their foe was determined to drive them to extinction because of the Huguenots' religious beliefs.[1]

As Paul struggled to establish churches throughout the Roman world, God led him to the most extraordinary couple described anywhere in Scripture. God's Spirit had broken through and united a Jew and a pagan Roman in Christian marriage. Unheard of! Outrageous! But Aquila and Priscilla, though probably outcasts from their own families because of their daring romance and marriage, were open to the dramatic moving of Holy Spirit. Priscilla was part of that tiny minority of upper-class Roman women who were as well educated as men. And she was gifted as a theologian, preacher, and church leader. Paul considered her his equal partner in the work of Christ. She was even willing to risk death for Paul's sake! And it is most important to grasp the idea that both Paul and Priscilla's husband, Aquila, were open to God's working in these unusual ways—an openness that is not characteristic of a lot of Christian men today.

According to Nancy Hardesty, there are numerous examples throughout Church history of God's breaking through social customs and using latter-day Priscillas in ways that made their male contemporaries sit up and pay attention.[2] One of these was Catherine of Siena. At age sixteen the young nun did what for her day was the scandalous thing of mixing in city crowds. She "visited prisons, attended executions to comfort the accused and their families, took food to the destitute, even shared her own clothes with the poor."[3] Later on, in even more scandalous and unheard-of behavior for a woman in her twenties, Catherine openly criticized popes, cardinals, and other male church leaders whom she thought were unfaithful to their mission.

In the early nineteenth century when it was inconceivable for single women to serve as missionaries, it was a woman who obeyed God and broke through social conventions to found the first interdenominational mission agency.[4] She was Sarah Doremus, called "the Mother of Missions."

And there is Catherine Booth, who, throughout the nineteenth century when women preachers, few in number, were savagely attacked by church leaders, nonetheless preached to thousands. Catherine Booth shattered society's conceptions of ministry to the downtrodden, and with the help of her husband, William, founded the Salvation Army.[5] She was probably one of the first Christians ever to recognize negotiation as the key to working out equal-partner marriages, because she rejected male leadership and would not marry any man who insisted on it. She once wrote to William that if a difference of opinion arose, "each should set forth their views and then either one would convince the other or a compromise would evolve."

And what of today? God's Spirit still wants to break through. There are the Harolds and the Alices and many like them who are doing unusual things to make their marriages both stable and stimulating. New and exciting patterns are available to those free enough to practice the kind of "radical" mutual submission necessary to create those patterns. Unfortunately, many marriages will be left out because the partners "already have all the answers," or else see no need for the examined marriage.

When's the last time you examined your marriage . . . your own views of it . . . your partner's views?

8.

NEGOTIATION IN
CHILD-REARING AND DATING

ALMOST ALL THE illustrations and examples in prior chapters have been about married persons. The principles and ideas in those chapters can and do apply equally to singles of any age, however. Learning how to negotiate creatively is not something "for marrieds only"; unmarried persons of the opposite sex also have to learn *how* to mutually submit to each other. The same is true, of course, among friends of the same sex. But single men and women face special problems in "relating" to each other that same-sex friends do not. The heart of the problem is that women and men have trouble being "just friends." Being male and female often gets in the way, and hierarchy is the same barrier to creative compromise and mutual submission for singles that it is for marrieds. The only way to scale the barrier is to replace males and females with people.

Some Christian singles like to address each other as "brother" and "sister" in order to convey the sense of family they share in Christ—a family that enables them to relate to each other primarily as human beings, as *persons* made in the image of God. This common bond goes a long way toward overcoming the artificial distinctions that society places upon us by labeling us as male and female. We all know that brothers and sisters treat each other very differently than unrelated males and females treat each other. Brothers and sisters treat each other as people, as friends. There is relatively little attempt to play the roles of "initiator" and "follower" that a secular society wants singles to play.

Dating Customs

One writer takes strong exception to Christian singles addressing one another as brother and sister. Why? "You don't want a *date* with a *brother*," she says. She tells us that having a Coke or a game of tennis with a brother "in the flesh" is very different from having the same things with a "guy." And what is a "guy"? A guy is a "man [who] sees a woman *as* a woman, not as a sister, not as a buddy or an equal, but as a potential wife." And why is the man, not the woman, doing the looking? Because, the writer says, God tells men to initiate and women to respond. Like Sigmund Freud, she believes that "submission is the essence of feminity," or being female. Assertiveness, she makes clear, is the essence of masculinity, or being male.

And what's so special about dating? "It's obvious that in our culture dating is a social situation which the man must initiate. . . . The girl doesn't ask him for the date. He asks; he decides where they're going and he pays the bills. . . . Obviously . . . she goes where he wants to go. . . . The whole idea of dating involves being a gentleman and being a lady. . . . Dating . . . is one way of expressing the God-given distinction between the sexes."[1]

To talk that way about dating is to imply that American dating and marriage customs are so special that they merit divine approval. But how do Christians in other societies feel about that? For example, do courtship customs in Jamaica, or Japan, or Iran have more or less divine approval than those in the United States? What about Mexico or Sweden, Zaire, or South

Africa? In much of India today young men and women do not "date," fall in love and marry. Instead their parents choose their mates for them, while the young persons themselves have only a veto over their parents' choices. Does that please God?

As a matter of fact in the Europe from which most Americans came, marriages were arranged in much the same way as they currently are in India, at least up through the eighteenth century. The hit musical *Fiddler on the Roof* centers on a late nineteenth-century clash between the ancient custom of arranged marriage and modern dating. The Bible knows nothing at all of modern dating customs. Instead the Old Testament supports the idea of parents choosing their children's mates for them, and not allowing them free choice (Gen. 24). The New Testament affirms the ancient command to obey our parents, and up until a century or two ago most Christians interpreted that to cover the choice of mates. If 22-year-old Jeremy wanted to marry 21-year-old Elizabeth, but his parents forbade it, Jeremy was supposed to obey them, out of obedience to God. The Moravian elders used the Lot (see p. 100) to help decide who should be allowed to marry whom. The idea that Christian youth should allow their parents to choose their mates has by no means expired; there are still some Christians who hold to this belief.

But which idea is truly God's will? Is it the relatively recent idea of the assertive man taking submissive "girls" on dates, paying their way, sorting them out, and then finally settling on one to follow and nurture him as he pursues the stormy path of life? Or is it the older idea of the man who asserts himself over women, but nonetheless submits himself to his parents? Thus when they instruct him as to whom he should or should not marry, he obeys.

Let's turn the question around. Is it possible that neither custom is God's will? Instead are not both customs merely pagan or secular? In fact, there is nothing particularly spiritual or sacred or divine or biblical about either of them, or about any other custom anywhere in the world. The irreducible biblical principle is that each person should obey God and marry the one whom he/she believes is God's choice for him/her (1 Cor. 7). Or if God wills it, that person should remain single. Whether God's will is revealed through parental choice (as it was expected to be years ago) or through contemporary dating patterns is totally immaterial. God is not chained by social customs. He works through, and often in spite of, whatever customs societies (people) devise.

Changes in Dating Customs

It is generally agreed that Christians seldom lead the rest of society into meaningful changes. Most Christians usually follow far off and accept changes long after the rest of society no longer considers them innovative. Besides the shift from arranged marriages to dating customs, two recent examples of Christians' ultimately accepting social trends are birth control and racial integration. It seems to me that the area of dating customs is one in which Christians can bring about exciting changes that the rest of society could follow. Although some secular observers have already roundly criticized American dating patterns, it isn't too late for that sort of leadership. On university campuses one can already detect evidence that dating as we have known it may *very slowly* be going the way of arranged-marriage customs. Since marriage itself appears to be changing it would seem odd indeed if premarriage customs were standing still.

How are Christians uniquely suited to leadership in changing premarital customs? Through their common kinship in Christ. Christian men and women are "family." As kinfolk they're free to relate as brothers and sisters, as human beings, as persons. In contrast, contemporary secular dating customs emphasize male-female differences, inequalities, and limitations.

A woman is limited if she can't ask a man friend to spend time with her. A man is likewise limited if he is embarrassed, ashamed, or uncomfortable to have a woman friend do just that. It is cheating a woman to say she can't experience the gratification of using her own money to do or buy things for a man. And pity the man who's never been on the receiving end of that sort of beneficence.

In chapter 1 I pointed out that as the years go by, many married women become bland. That process begins prior to marriage as they are denied the right to take the initiative in proposing what to do, where to go, and how to spend time with their men friends. Men likewise miss much of the richness that could be theirs if women were their equals in deciding how best to "invest" time together.

A great poverty of soul, mind, and spirit comes from the idea that men and women who spend time together must think of themselves primarily as potential marriage partners. That pre-occupation keeps them from unlocking all the benefits of per-sonhood and pure friendship that each can give and receive *right now*. But the greatest tragedy of dating as it is commonly prac-ticed is that it does not enable adolescents or single adults to practice Paul's words "to submit to one another." "Proper" dating behavior makes it difficult for the male to negotiate in the manner described in prior chapters. Ditto for the female.

Moving Toward "Friending"

What practical things can we do to help adolescents and single adults to shift from dating to what we might call "friend-ing"? Parents of singles, pastors and other leaders interested in singles' welfare, and single adolescents and adults themselves know that such changes are not going to occur without a lot of struggle and pain. High school students in particular feel intense peer pressure to conform to secular dating customs. Therefore, whatever is introduced to encourage adolescents (as well as older singles) to "friend" rather than date has to be done gradually and slowly. We're dealing with customs that have been around for two hundred years. They're not going to change overnight.

Child Training and Dating

One vital thing that parents can do to change such customs is to examine the ways in which they train their children. If parents train their girls to play a feminine, submissive role toward boys, and if they train boys to play a masculine, assertive role toward girls, then dating as we know it (as well as marriages in which the husband is head) will be around for a long time to come. Instead, parents must begin by getting their children to *think* about male-female relations. *Why* do singles (adolescents or adults) do what they do? Is there a better way to it? Underlying that questioning of dating customs, and fundamental to it, is how parents train their children—girls and boys—to negotiate.

As the young child develops, the parents *deal* with the child. The child learns from the parents and *deals* with them in the same way they deal with him. Psychologist Dr. Thomas Gordon, for example, in his book *Parent Effectiveness Training*, refers to three methods of dealing with children when conflicts arise between them and parents. In Method I, the parent decides on a solution to the conflict, announces it to the child and hopes s/he will accept it. If the child does not, the parent tries to persuade him/her to accept. "If this fails the parent usually tries to get compliance by employing power and authority." [2] In this method the parent wins and the child loses—the child is *made* to do something s/he would rather not do.

Under Method II, the parent may or may not have a preconceived solution to the conflict. If s/he does, s/he tries to persuade the child to accept it, while simultaneously the child tries to get the parent to accept his/her preconceived solution. If the parent resists, the child controls the parent by temper tantrums, making the parent feel guilty and saying "nasty, deprecating things" to him or her.[3] Finally, the parent "gives in." The parent loses, the child wins.

While there are many reasons that both methods are unacceptable, the main one is this: in neither case does the child learn the art of mutual submission. The child fails to grasp the importance of love and the passion for justice referred to in earlier chapters. S/he is cheated out of the satisfying experience of mutual give-and-take. The child does not discover how enriching it can be to face challenges in the form of a conflict or disagreement and then patiently persevere until it is resolved to the mutual satisfaction of both parties. The kinds of negotiation strategies mentioned in prior chapters are simply foreign to the child's existence. Instead, the child is either forced to conform without active participation in the resolution of the conflict (Method I); or else is allowed to exercise a kind of mini-tyranny over his/her parents (Method II).

If we were to take a scientific survey of *Christian* homes, it is certain we would discover that only a handful would prefer to raise their children under Method II. The majority would prefer Method I. In recent years, certain seminars have been held nationwide that advocate that the Method I approach to child-rearing is *the* Christian way. Donald Schroeder is a minister who has attended those seminars and also *Gordon's Parent Effectiveness Training* (PET) sessions.[4] Schroeder summarizes the Method I seminars' principles of child training in these ways.

Family. The father is the head of the family and makes the rules. The child must abdicate his own rights to follow and obey the parent's will.

Rights. "Those who would insist on their own rights are breeding anger and worry. To solve those twin problems . . .

family members . . . come under the direction of the power of the father (this is called chain of command)."

Discipline. Parents should instruct so as to gain obedience from children; warn them; clarify their instructions; correct the child by *breaking his/her will* but not spirit.

Dating. The boy should ask the girl's father for permission to date his daughter. There are prescribed qualities for the boy, and the girl's father is responsible for the boy's character-building. The seeds of marriage breakdown can be traced to failure to carry out chain-of-command principles while dating.

In contrast to this approach, Gordon comes up with Method III, the "no lose" method for resolving parent-child conflicts. An adaptation of Gordon specifically for Christian parents is found in the book *You Can Have a Family Where Everybody Wins.*[5] Instead of trying to "break the child's will," the idea is to make the child a *willing* participant in decisions that affect him/her and other family members. Under Method III, "each unique parent and his/her unique child can solve each of their unique conflicts by finding their own unique solutions acceptable to both."[6]

Parent-Child Joint Profit

You will immediately recognize that this method is exactly the same thing as the maximum joint profit idea we talked about in earlier chapters. Joint profit or the well-being of all parties concerned means that wives and husbands learn to negotiate creative compromises that are fair for both of them. These compromises should simultaneously promote the interests of each of them, as well as their marriage/family as a whole. Each spouse has the responsibility to point out the selfish goals and self-seeking strategies of the other. Mutual submission instead of male authority becomes the central feature of the wife-husband relationship.

Similarly (since in Ephesians 5: 21 Paul made no excep

tions) mutual submission instead of ultimate parental power becomes the central feature of the parent-child relationship. Obviously, the pivotal difference between parent-child and husband-wife relationships is the *age* of the child. Up to a certain age, parents are accountable both to God and society (the law) for how their children behave. But sometime between ages 18–21, every state releases the parent from that accountability. And at some less precise stage of the mature offspring's development, parents cease to be accountable to God for what their sons and daughters do. Like the parents of the blind man who was being attacked by religious leaders because he did not conform to their authority, there comes a time when every parent must say, "Ask him [to account for his/her own actions], s/he is of age, s/he will speak for him/her self" (John 9: 21).

However, relinquishing accountability does not mean that God will not hold parents responsible for what they did while the child was under the age of maturity. It is during those formative and fleeting years that parents set the tone of their dealings with their children. While Method II is an unacceptable way to deal with children, so is Method I. Method I produces boys and girls that will deal with each other by imitating their hierarchal home situations.

Boys will assume that since their fathers make the rules that govern relationships with women, they should do the same during the dating period—subject of course to the "higher rules" of the girl's father. Once married, however, the ultimacy of the father's rules over the girl are replaced by the ultimacy of the boy's (now her husband's) rules. Simultaneously, Method I teaches girls that they can make little if any creative input that will effectively *change* their parents', their boyfriend's, or their husband's behaviors. Ultimately, they must do the adjusting, the conforming, the significant changing—both during dating and in marriage. Marriage means that they are transferred from being somebody's daughter to being somebody's wife. They never are nor do they become their *own autonomous person* before God.

It is true that a boy growing up under some form of Method I conforms rigorously to his parents' wishes with little opportunity for effective participation (negotiation) in the decisions that affect his life. Nevertheless, realizing two things keeps him from being squelched completely. These things keep his will from actually being "broken," as described above.

One, he can exercise at least some degree of leadership, initiative, and authority over girls that he dates. Second, he knows that someday he will be out from under his parents' control and in control of his own family. Instead of being at the bottom of the chain of command, he will be at the top. Instead of being "struck" by a hammer and chisel he will do the striking. While the boy is learning to be assertive, he is not absorbing what it means to submit to a female peer. He never learns to practice the dynamics of Method III with an equal who "happens" to be a woman.

In contrast, a woman growing up under Method I has much less opportunity either in present or future to exercise initiative and leadership. Her will indeed becomes "broken." Dating customs, high school youth groups, and many campus organizations often discourage active women's leadership. If she contemplates marriage, that only promises her more of what her parental family is like—isolation from being an active participant in effective negotiations arrived at through achieving justice and "fair play."

I feel very strongly that both sexes are cheated when they do not learn to relate to each other under a Method III style. Men, just as much as women, suffer a certain shallowness as a result of this kind of deprivation. And it is a deprivation as surely as some children are deprived of economic and cultural opportunities. Like these other deprivations, the consequences follow them all their lives. But also like these other deprivations, those consequences can be reversed. Adult singles caught in the "dating game" can get out of it and enter into "friending relationships." However, before we look at that matter, let's first consider the situation of parents struggling to use Method III with their children ("everybody wins") instead of being trapped by Method I ("parent wins, child loses").

Training Children for Participation in Decisions

The child's age is a key factor, as we have noted. The younger the child, the more often parents will have to act in a unilateral manner simply to keep the child from physical harm or danger. But where the child's safety is not at stake, the child is never too young to begin dealing with him/her in terms of Gordon's six steps.[7]

1. Identify and define the conflict.
2. Generate possible alternative solutions.
3. Evaluate the alternative solutions.
4. Decide on the best acceptable solution.
5. Work out ways to implement the solution.
6. Follow up to evaluate how it worked.

It's not necessary to go into great detail as to *how* to work out these steps since that's already been done in prior chapters.[8] The *how* of parent-child negotiation is basically the same as the how of wife-husband negotiations. Open communication is essential to this style, especially in discovering what the issue or conflict really is (point 1). Does the child want to play over at a friend's house; take dancing lessons; participate in a certain sport? For some reason, does the parent object? Why? What does the parent want the child to start or stop doing? Get the disagreements out in the open. That can be done with children from preschoolers on up as long as the parent communicates on the child's level.

Points 2 and 3 are simply ways to carry on creative compromise. Here the parent can perform an enormously important function of teaching the child to be creative in thinking of the most imaginative ways to solve differences. And the child can learn that what is "best" (point 4) means what is *best for both* parent and child, not just one or the other. Points 4 and 5 include the dynamics of negotiation, the nuts and bolts of mutual submission, of actually hammering out a compromise that both can live with. Once again the parent does the child an enormous service by teaching the child how to give in, *as well as how to take,* in a context of love and justice. The child learns to settle for less than s/he originally wanted, and learns that the parent is willing to do the same thing.

In earlier chapters we saw how easy it is for persons to renege or forget agreements they have made. That's why point 6 is so important for children to grasp. They should learn that they have the right to remind their parents of past agreements, just as parents have the same right towards them. Underlying these six steps is the idea that whenever a parent or child has a disagreement or conflict with the other, these are the ways to be used to resolve it. The parent tries to resist the temptation to fall back on Method I, especially after the child reaches the teen years. That temptation is resisted as strongly as a husband such as Harold resists the urge to act as "final authority" over his wife Alice.

Realistically, it's probably too much to expect that all parents will always be able to resist Method I and to pursue III instead. Following those six steps is much harder work than simply telling the child what to do. As one gentleman told me in a church where I was leading a seminar on these matters, "It's so much simpler just to have wives and children obey." Nevertheless, our goal should be to make joint participation in decision-making (Method III) the prevailing and pervasive style of dealing with our children. In particular, Method III should be followed whenever a major issue arises in the child's life. By major, I mean things like behavior at school, study habits, peer relations, employment, church and related activities, leisure activities, and household chores.

Child Training and Friending

An important outcome of Method III style is that parents can easily encourage their adolescents of both sexes to "friend," rather than date.[9] In a context of mutual give-and-take about all matters, it is very natural for parents to say, "Look, the way we relate to you is the way you should relate to boys/girls." (It is to be hoped that the parents will also set an example by maintaining a Method III style between themselves.)

Very likely, the child reared with Method III would not want it any other way. The girl who grew up with Method III will feel that she does not want to play the "dating game" with a boy who does not recognize her first as a person, and only incidentally as female. She wants him to acknowledge her participation as a full and equal partner in all decisions that govern how they will spend their time together. She doesn't become subordinate when she spends time with other girls; why should she do so with boys?

Similarly, the boy who grew up with Method III will not want to play the "game" with girls who are not prepared to take on equal responsibilities. He wants the enrichment that comes from her inputs, and from negotiating creative solutions when they have disagreements. The Method III boy wants a full and free person for a friend, just as much as the Method III girl wants to be that kind of person. Let me reemphasize: the girl's inputs to a friending relationship are essentially no different from a boy's inputs, and include the freedom to ask any boy at any time to spend time with her, as well as the freedom to bear part or all of the financial costs involved.

It does not take a crystal ball to realize that as yet there are not many "free" adolescents of that sort to be found. But there are probably more of them today than there were ten years ago. Ten years from now their numbers will probably have increased still more. Should a free adolescent who can't find another free adolescent refuse to "date"? That's something each person must answer individually. One workable solution might be to date, but then begin to transform the other person's traditional ideas so that the relationship becomes a "friending" one. That requires skillful negotiation, but it can be done, especially if the other individual is basically an "open" person—a person who welcomes exciting, innovative, and important change.

9.

NEGOTIATION
FOR ADULT SINGLES

WE SHIFT OUR focus now to adult singles—people beyond high school, whether they are working or in college or vocational school. Both Jesus and Paul had a great deal of positive things to say about singleness (Matt. 19 and 1 Cor. 7). A recent book shows how rich a life singles can have in contemporary society.[1] There are many ways in which Christian singles can serve God much more effectively than marrieds.

The Risk of a Mismatch

Singleness is incomparably preferable to a marriage in which the man wants to be the head of the household, but the woman wants an equal-partner arrangement. The same is true in those fewer but evidently increasing cases where the husband wants an equal partner—a full person—but ends up with a traditional wife. In either situation the possibility of the kinds of deadlocks we talked about in earlier chapters greatly increases. When each has different ground rules as to what marriage is all about it becomes much more difficult for wives and husbands to resolve disagreements in a way that is fair and acceptable to both.

The egalitarian woman or man sees strong, healthy marriages to be the union of two persons who develop their God-given abilities and potentials to the full. The marriage becomes a dynamic context that stimulates *each* partner to be more than s/he could be had s/he remained single. Differences are negotiated with that grand objective in mind. The outcome is stable and satisfying marriages.

In contrast, the man or woman who believes in some form of male headship is less concerned about full development of free persons than in conformity to a set of given rules that, ultimately, are enforced by the husband. "Freedom" says one spokesman for hierarchy, "is not the right to do what we want, but the power to do what we ought." [2] For the married woman in such a relationship, freedom means the power to obey her husband who decides what she *ought* to do.

The grievous problems inherent in that sort of male ultimacy have been dealt with in detail in the foregoing chapters. The point here is that any woman who believes that freedom is the right to explore fully everything God has for her, who believes her prime allegiance is to God and not to any man (Acts 5: 29), is going to be hard pressed to negotiate justice with a husband who tells her the essence of her freedom is to submit to his initiatives. Therefore, any such single woman who becomes the least bit "interested" in a man is well-advised to "test" him. Among other things, she might ask him to read this book and begin to discuss with him the kinds of issues it raises. Find out which view of marriage, which view of freedom he holds. When disagreements arise, discover while you're still single whether or not he's ever learned how to negotiate for the maximum benefit of both of you. Can he negotiate the way Harold did in chapters 3 and 4? If he doesn't know how, is he willing to learn? Are both of you willing to learn and struggle together over conflict-resolution? Does he understand what you mean when you say you want to marry a "friend," not a traditional husband? Does he share Gibran's vision of friendship as caught in the verse from the preface?

If the answers to the last several questions are positive, the way is clear to keep on exploring whether God wants you to marry him. If the answers are negative, the yellow caution light is on and you proceed at your own risk. In fact, marriage is risky even if you say, "I'm a traditional woman and I want to marry a traditional man." It's risky because even though you're traditional at marriage, it's possible that you'll change your views about male headship after a few years of marriage. Remember chapter 7—change is life's only constant. There is research evidence showing that after being married for several years, some women become less traditional about male headship.[3] Apparently they find that headship doesn't work as well as they thought it would, and so they begin to question it. As indicated in chapter 1, some Christian leaders are changing their views about male headship.[4] They are trying to make the idea softer, more palatable, less onerous. The direction is plain. Just as Christians gradually learned, for instance, to accept birth control, they are already learning to "work at" and "work out" egalitarian marriages. In other words, any woman who marries today thinking she is content to let her "head" prescribe her "oughts," may wake up tomorrow and discover some "oughts" of her own which she'd like to suggest but which he resists.

It is, however, by no means impossible for a married woman to negotiate justice with her husband, even if he is traditional. The principles described in earlier chapters are designed to accomplish that very thing regardless of the husband's (or wife's) views of male headship. Nevertheless, let's face it—mutual submission (negotiation) will be harder work where the couple differs over the headship principle.

The Single Man: Benefits and Opportunity

Just as a single woman who wants to marry a friend should explore premarital negotiations, a single man who wants a friend should do likewise. The motivation behind wanting to marry a friend rather than a traditional wife is the same as wanting a friend instead of a traditional husband. As suggested throughout this book, a marriage based on friendship will be much richer and more satisfying for *both* partners—the man as well as the woman. Someone has said that many traditional marriages are held together by "quiet desperation." What the single man who favors the headship idea doesn't realize is that he will be cheating himself. My feminist friends will pardon the following property analogy, but a hierarchical approach to marriage makes it appropriate: It's as if a man were to obtain a Jaguar automobile with all of its power, beauty, grace, and elegance, and then keep it in the garage except for a weekly round trip to the grocery store in the next block. Not only would the car suffer, the man himself would be poorer for having made the investment and not reaping from it all the benefits and pleasure he possibly could.

That's exactly what happens in a traditional marriage. A man receives a gift of power and beauty, grace and elegance—and more: intelligence, wisdom, and a creature made in the image of God with the potential to create more than just babies.[5] But the traditional husband puts her in the garage—under the umbrella or mantle of his headship—and never reaps from her all the benefits and pleasure he could. Not only is he cheated, so are their children, as well as the church, community, and society.

The way to avoid those losses is to forget the property analogy. The single man should not be "dating" and trying to unearth a "female" who will be "subject" to his initiative and leadership. Instead he should be "friending," and searching for a person who is his equal and to whom he can submit, as well as she to him. Why should he do that? Because the woman will be better off if he does? Yes—that's the "passion for justice" I mentioned in chapter 3. But equally vital, perhaps even more important from his standpoint, *he* will be better off if he does. *He* will have richer premarital experiences; *he* will have a richer marriage.

Why? Because in the first place, she will be free to *bring to him* all that she is and has, without fear that her selfhood will be stifled if it does not fit into his "oughts" for her. Second, she will be free to create *together with him* through the dynamics of joint and equal decision-making, a marriage more satisfying and more beneficial to him than he could otherwise have had if he were the "head" or "leader" or "prime initiator." In the first instance, the woman is less likely to become the "bland blah" that men over thirty like to tell jokes about. She is more likely to keep on becoming more and more of her own person whom her husband can admire in her own right— and not merely as an extension of himself. And not only will she keep alive and growing and thus be a growing pleasure to her husband; in the second instance, the whole marriage itself will be kept alive and growing and thus be an increasing pleasure to him as much as to her.

Very often Christians will say to me, "Are not wives supposed to be subject to their husbands in the same way that humans are to be subject to Christ?" The verses on which they base that question have been exegeted elsewhere [6] so I don't need to go into them here. But let me add that Jesus tells us we are no longer slaves but friends (John 15: 15). The Catechism tells us that the "chief end" of humans is to "enjoy God and glorify him forever." How do we enjoy God? How does he enjoy us? The enjoyment grows out of the struggle to know and do his will, and thus coming to know him more intimately (Phil. 3: 8–14). The newness and freshness of the Christian experience develop out of the process of becoming like Christ.

In marriage terms, the male is not God—he is hardly infallible nor omniscient nor omnipotent. The fallible man joins forces with the fallible woman, and together they submit to each other in order to learn more perfectly how to submit to Christ and become like him. In short, a man's own spiritual life and growth and development are likely to be greater where he learns the humility of submission than where he continues to insist on the pride of male headship. What greater incentive could there be for men to seek the kind of friend who can do that much for them?

An additional, though unfortunate, fact to keep in mind is that at present it's simpler for men than for women to take the lead in friending. Though we wish it were not so, centuries of secular tradition have taught men to be leaders and women to be followers. Only with great effort do contemporary women struggle to achieve the biblical ideal that "holy boldness" should characterize every Christian, regardless of sex. Though more are doing so than ever before, it remains difficult for single women, whether adolescent or adult, to take the initiative and challenge dating stereotypes.

And though such challenges are not simple for men to make, it still remains less difficult for them to do so. Therefore, at this point in history if a man (adolescent or adult) begins to shape his relationship with a woman so as to develop a friending relationship, the chances are she is more likely to allow herself to be shaped than is a man whom the woman is trying to convert into a friend.

Christian men then have a unique opportunity, privilege, and responsibility to exercise leadership and bring about extremely important changes that will benefit individuals, family, church, and society. The times have never been more ripe for such leadership. Should faint hearts await a more propitious time, the opportunity for leadership will have been frittered away, and Christians will once again find themselves following in the wake of "safe" patterns, as they almost always do. If Christian men are actually the leaders they say they are, we have never had a better time to prove it!

EPILOG

MUCH MORE COULD be said about creative conflict between women and men, parents and children. We have only begun to scratch the surface. Each of these chapters could be expanded into a book of its own. It is to be hoped that these ever-expanding chapters will be written by our daily lives, as increasing numbers of Christians struggle to put mutual submission into practice.

Underlying the information and ideas contained throughout these chapters is something else I trust the book conveys—a tone, a spirit, a vision, a desire, a conviction. What I'm talking about is difficult to express, but its essence is this: There may be differing opinions over many of the specific points discussed throughout these pages. Some readers, for instance, may feel that particular negotiating techniques are more appropriate than others in trying to resolve certain types of conflicts. Those informational points can be settled by more and more practice.

Yet practice takes place where there is a spirit and conviction on the part of Christians that "this is the way to go." As more and more Christians catch that "vision of marriage" I discussed in chapter 7, I believe they will want very strongly to practice mutual submission. I believe they will want to increase their negotiating effectiveness—effectiveness in reaching agreements that are fair, equitable, and just for all parties concerned.

That is the loving thing to do. But it is also the difficult thing to do because of past experiences in which we have approached man-woman (parent-child) relations in the wrong tone or spirit. We have been convinced that harmony, beauty, tranquility, and order are somehow achieved through the male acting as a unique agent of God. May God grant us grace to catch a new spirit, a new tone—one in which we perceive that beauty and strength emerge from women and men acting together as equal partners to please and serve God in the world.

NOTES

PREFACE

1. Letha Scanzoni and Nancy Hardesty, *All We're Meant to Be* (Waco, Tex.: Word Books, 1974); Virginia Mollenkott, *Women, Men, and the Bible* (Nashville: Abingdon, 1977).
2. George R. Bach and Peter Wyden, *The Intimate Enemy: How to Fight Fair in Love and Marriage* (New York: William Morrow, 1969); Sherod Miller et al, *Alive and Aware: Improving Communications in Relationships* (Minneapolis: Interpersonal Communications, 1975); George R. Bach and Ronald M. Deutsch, *Pairing* (New York: Avon, 1975).

CHAPTER 1

1. In the former instance, see Marabel Morgan, *The Total Woman* (Old Tappan, N.J.: Fleming H. Revell, 1973). One representative of the second view is Elisabeth Elliot, who writes in *His* magazine, January 1978, "I have no doctrinal quarrels with Marabel. The only objections I would raise to her book would be purely matters of taste" (pp. 23–24).
2. Letha Scanzoni and Nancy Hardesty, *All We're Meant to Be;* Virginia Mollenkott, *Women, Men and the Bible;* Paul K. Jewett,

Male as Male and Female (Grand Rapids: Eerdmans, 1975).

3. We see a striking illustration of "hurt" in chapter 6 through Andy's behavior toward his wife, Dana, and his daughter, Jill.

4. Joseph Durso, "Yankees, Old and New," *New York Times,* Sunday, August 14, 1977.

5. Fritz Ridenour, "Let's Not Be Glib about Lib," *Family Life Today,* vol. 1, no. 2, January 1975, p. 1.

6. Fritz Ridenour, "They're My Groceries, Too," *Family Life Today,* vol. 4, no. 3, February 1978, pp. 8–10.

CHAPTER 2

1. Horatius Bonar, "Go, Labour On."

2. Recall that C. S. Lewis in *The Great Divorce* (New York: Macmillan, 1946) suggested that even after death persons who had not become believers during their lifetimes would be uninterested in doing so afterward.

CHAPTER 3

1. Sandy Dengler, "Cold War," *Family Life Today,* vol. 4, no. 2, January 1978, pp. 14–15.

2. Quotation attributed to Mrs. Elizabeth Handford (a daughter of John R. Rice) in a public lecture given in Richmond, Virginia, as reported by Mary Anne Pikrone in the *Richmond News Leader,* October 22, 1977, p. 3.

3. Ibid.

4. Ibid.

5. Roberty E. Tomasson, "Man and Wife Ordained Priests in Episcopal Ritual in Danbury," *New York Times,* December 18, 1977, p. 45.

6. See Stanlee Phelps and Nancy Austin, *The Assertive Woman* (Fredericksburg, Va.: Impact, 1975), and Pamela Butler, *Self-Assertion for Women* (New York: Harper & Row, 1976).

CHAPTER 4

1. See the essay by Elin Schoen on several "two-career" couples in *New York* magazine, vol. 9, no. 43, October 25, 1976.
2. See note 2, chap. 1.

CHAPTER 5

1. A. E. R. Boak and W. G. Sinnigen, *A History of Rome to A.D. 565* (New York: Macmillan, 1965).
2. John Scanzoni, *Sex Roles, Women's Work and Marital Conflict* (Lexington, Mass.: D. C. Heath, Lexington Books, 1978).
3. See, for example, Elisabeth Elliot, in *His* magazine, November 1977, p. 1.
4. Ibid.

CHAPTER 6

1. Hunter James, *Old Salem: Official Guidebook* (Winston-Salem, N.C.: Old Salem, Inc., 1977), p. 8.

CHAPTER 7

1. Nancy Hardesty, "Two Queens Aid the French Revolution," *Eternity,* January 1975, pp. 44–47.
2. See her series in the 1974–75 issues of *Eternity.*
3. Nancy Hardesty, "Catherine of Siena—Luther's Predecessor," *Eternity,* December 1974, pp. 38–39.
4. Nancy Hardesty, "Sarah Doremus—Mother of Missions," *Eternity,* April 1975, pp. 45–47.
5. Nancy Hardesty, "Catherine Booth, Co-Founder of the Salvation Army," *Eternity,* May 1975, pp. 52–54.

CHAPTER 8

1. Elisabeth Elliot, *His* magazine, November 1975. See also *His* magazine, January 1978, "A *His* Interview with Elisabeth Elliott."
2. Thomas Gordon, *Parent Effectiveness Training* (New York: P. H. Wyden Co., 1970), p. 153.
3. Ibid., p. 159.
4. Donald Schroeder, "Biblical and Theological Tie-Ins with P.E.T.," unpublished paper, First Presbyterian Church, Wichita, Kansas, 1975.
5. By Earl H. Gaulke (St. Louis: Concordia Press, 1975).
6. Gordon, op. cit., p. 200.
7. Ibid., p. 237.
8. Also read Gordon; and Gaulke.
9. See Joan Huyser, "Of Olive Plants and Dates," *Reformed Journal,* June 1978. This essay also tries to break us out of "the dating habit."

CHAPTER 9

1. Margaret Adams, *Single Blessedness* (New York: Basic Books, 1976).
2. Quoted by Schroeder, loc. cit.
3. Scanzoni, 1978, loc. cit.
4. See also Joseph Bayly, *Eternity,* March 1975.
5. This in no way denigrates child-bearing or caring. The point is that women can do many things *besides* bear children. And both men and women can care for them equally well.
6. See note 2, chap. 1.

	DATE DUE		